THE CUBAN AMERICAN EXPERIENCE

THE CUBAN AMERICAN EXPERIENCE: ISSUES, PERCEPTIONS, AND REALITIES

BY GUARIONE M. DIAZ

REEDY PRESS
St. Louis, Missouri

Reedy Press
PO Box 5131, St. Louis, MO 63139, USA

Library of Congress Control Number: 2006940121

ISBN: 978-1-933370-11-8
       1-933370-11-4

For all information on all Reedy Press publications visit our website at www.reedypress.com.

Printed in the United States of America
07 08 09 10 11 5 4 3 2 1

This book is dedicated to the nice American. If an ugly American exists, as books and movies tell us, then there must be a nice American as well. In fact, I have been privileged to meet quite a lot of them.

Whether refugees, parolees, or rafters, Cuban Americans have had firsthand knowledge of many nice Americans. They are the ones who save lives in the high seas or craft policies allowing refugees to come to America: the ones who show their generosity to newcomers they have never met.

This nice American is the embodiment of a hard-working people who live quietly and unassumingly in thousands of communities, each different, but all American: of the millions of Americans of all creeds, colors, and countries of origin who love peace but stand ready to uphold and defend the principles this nation was built upon.

My sincere gratitude to the nice American.

CONTENTS

PREFACE

The Cuban Revolution and much of Cuba's previous history are complex and a subject of continued debate among Cubans and non-Cubans alike.

Both are often seen through a mix of stereotypes, deep-felt emotions and beliefs, and superficial knowledge of historical developments. In the case of Cuban Americans, cross-cultural issues and internal differences and contradictions among Cuban Americans themselves complicate perceptions even more.

To illustrate this case, let's suppose someone looked at Cuban Americans for the first time. He or she would see a community of unyielding exiles who savor small symbolic victories against Castro's regime, mixed with thousands of immigrants yearning for social freedom and a chance to build a future; individuals who after claiming political asylum visit Cuba regularly and return unharmed; a community perceived as immigrant of which one third of its members were U.S. born.

This is a community often represented by some who fled Cuba seeking freedom of speech but cannot understand why Castro sympathizers, or those without strong feelings against him, should be allowed to express themselves publicly, a community that tends to stay within itself but can't figure out why others don't understand them; one that adjusts well to and generally succeeds in the U.S. while holding tight to its culture and native language; a significant voting bloc that influences America's political process but is occasionally ignored by presidential candidates; a small conglomerate, when compared to the U.S. population, but with a sizeable number of top-rated mainstream entertainers, corporate CEOs, university presidents, major league athletes, elected and appointed public officials, writers, and artists; a group of immigrants perceived as newcomers but who in areas like Miami are the largest ethnic/ national group residing in the city.

Most Cubans oppose Castro but are divided on how to deal with him. They are glued to Cuba news but most will stay in the U.S. after Castro is gone; they are a community that places family unity over political differences but fights to keep a child away from his father in order that he can live a better life in a democratic society; a community where early upper-strata refugees continuously welcome and integrate newcomers into it and help them settle in the U.S. regardless of age, race, religion, social background, and increasing cultural nuances.

This is the Cuban American community: all at once, simple and complex, global and parochial, young and old, Cuban American and American Cuban, for years to come.

To analyze the impact of the Cuban Revolution on the Cuban American community in a historical context inevitably leaves much to be told. This book has been written for a general readership, but with American college students and second and third generations of Cuban Americans in mind. I hope too that it will provide the general public with an introduction to and a source of consultation on Cuban Americans. Hence, this book should be read as a synopsis of the Cuban American experience in the United States consisting of a chronicle of events, an analysis of facts, a summary of data, and a community portrait. It purports to offer a context for the Cuban American exodus from their homeland and their adjustment patterns in the U.S. It is written in a mostly non-academic format, except when technical terms or concepts are necessary, and seeks to present facts, analyses, and thoughts as fluently as possible. Admittedly, the chapters that follow do not provide the depth and historical detail of more voluminous and rigorous publications, and I hope that those interested will consult some of these sources.

ACKNOWLEDGMENTS

Over several decades, I have received valuable facts and opinions about Cuba from hundreds of friends and acquaintances. My apologies to those not mentioned below or in this bibliography.

I must start by thanking Father Mario Vizcaino, who encouraged me to move to Miami from New York in order to head the Cuban American National Council and become an active member of the U.S. Hispanic community.

More recently, I asked some friends about a few specific topics. They were open and generous in discussing them with me.

Willy Allen and Maria Rubio were helpful in reviewing the experiences of Cuban Americans in Miami and in sharing family military anecdotes dating back to the 1940s. The facts, figures, and interpretations I received from Oscar Baisman, Bernardo Benes, and Rafael Kravic allowed me to summarize the recent experiences of Cuban-Hebrews in the U.S.

I thank Jorge Sanguinetty for his many anecdotes on the revolution's early Economic Plans, as well as for other valuable academic and historical insights.

Likewise, Juan Benemelis, Adolfo Rivero Caro, and Ricardo Bofill shared with me their unique sojourns in Cuba's political and communist circles.

Armando Salas Amaro could not have been more generous in recalling the exile experience of Cuban Masons as he showed me the Halls of Miami's Great Masonic Temple. I learned from and enjoyed our meeting well beyond the scope of this book.

A student of Spain's history and its former role as Metropolis of the Americas, Ricardo Martinez Cid helped me frame the cultural interactions among Spain, England, and the U.S. and their respective influences in the development of Cuban culture.

The unpublished manuscript on the Bay of Pigs readily shared with me by Pablo Perez Cisneros allowed me to use precise figures and first-hand descriptions of this pivotal episode in the histories of Cuba, the U.S., and the Cuban American community.

Several long conversations with the Reverend Marcos Antonio Ramos gave me not only multiple insights about religion in pre-Castro Cuba—especially Protestantism—but also excellent suggestions for additional interviews and reading materials. My true appreciation to Lorenzo de Toro and Ondina Garcia Menocal, who provided me with institutional data on Cuban American Catholics.

I was privileged to look at Black Cuban Americans from three different perspectives, one of an average Black Cuban American family who arrived from Cuba in recent years; a second from a descendant of a family who co-founded the first social club of Cuban-Blacks in Tampa in the 1800s; and thirdly, from a respected academic ranked among the top experts on Afro-Cuban religion in the world. My sincere gratitude to Ines and Victor Piedra, to Gil Casellas, and to Mercedes Sandoval.

During several conversations with Ricardo Nuñez Portuondo, I reviewed some facts and figures on the former Cuban Refugee Program, which he directed during its last years. My sincere appreciation for his insights and recollections.

Arturo Estopiñan a top expert on Miami's political world was very generous in reviewing and commenting the chapter on Cuban American politics.

My thanks to Aida Levitan for her editorial advice and to Tom Boswell, a colleague in numerous research projects on Cuban Americans for comments on the Demography chapter.

I cannot thank enough George Foyo, Jorge Espinosa, and Arturo Torres for their confidence and advice since the early stages of my writing. Also, a very special thanks to David Gonzales from PepsiCo, Cirabel Olson from Burger King

Corporation, Jeanie Hernandez from Comcast, Sonia Green from General Motors Corporation, and Raquel Egusquiza from Ford Motors Company Fund for their financial support. My thanks to Cesar Pizarro and Liza Gross from *The Miami Herald* for providing me with information I used in the preparation of this book.

Completing several drafts would have been so much harder had it not been for the patience, skills, and disposition of my assistant Cristina Santana, who often managed to guess not only what I actually wrote but also what I really intended to say.

As usual, I must thank my wife Teresita and my daughter Susana for underscoring the roughness of my first draft. And my daughter Cristina for her thorough editing of the second. Leo Estrada's review of the manuscript was precise, insightful, and very useful as is customary with his work.

I have much to thank Raymond Garcia for his advice and guidance so essential to making the book more comprehensive and accessible to a broader readership.

Of course, all of the book's omissions and flaws are entirely my responsibility.

INTRODUCTION

The high profile of Cuban American émigrés is disproportionate to the size of the Cuban American community and to the island of Cuba. Political and migratory issues covered in Chapters 4 and 7 surrounding Cuban Americans have triggered a number of specific, often controversial policies by several administrations and congresses. Cuban Americans have also been influential in the election of governors and legislative bodies and more recently in the election of the president of the U.S.

Although it focuses on Cuban Americans in the U.S., Chapter 3 points to a succession of events dating back to the eighteenth century that help explain the long-term relationship between Cuba and the U.S., Florida in particular. It relates why Cubans seek to come to the U.S. and concomitantly why Cubans have been important to the U.S. during times of crisis.

Admittedly, I have a point of view about Cuba, the island where I was born. I lived there for twenty years and attended the University of Havana during the first three years of the Cuban Revolution.

For the last forty years, I have spent thousands of hours studying Cuba and Cuban Americans. I have held conversations with experts on Cuba. They include protagonists of the Cuban Revolution and recent arrivals from many different backgrounds and persuasions. The opportunities came as a result of my role as president of the Cuban American National Council (CNC), my efforts in the resettlement of Mariel refugees/entrants, and my work as civilian liaison, or ombudsman, of the U.S. government, at our naval base in Guantanamo, Cuba, during the rafters' interment

1

of 1994–95. Likewise, my active participation for three decades in Cuban American affairs has connected me with Cuban Americans and Hispanic communities throughout the U.S., and with top-ranked academics and researchers on Cuban American topics. Through these connections and through my years of residence in Florida, New Jersey, and New York, which host the three largest Cuban American communities in the U.S., I gained firsthand experience on a topic central to my life since the summer of 1961, the year I arrived. In most of its chapters, this book discusses Cuban Americans' relationship to both Hispanics and Americans in general. Chapter 1 offers a broad perspective of today's Hispanic community in the U.S.

In covering the Cuban American community in the U.S., the following pages treat Miami-Dade County Cuban Americans extensively for several reasons. First, this area contains the largest numbers and the largest concentration of Cuban Americans in any U.S. jurisdiction. Second, Miami-Dade is widely recognized as the hub for Cuban American media outlets and cultural events. It's the place where Cuban Americans as a group have the greatest and most visible political and economic impact. Finally, there is more data on Cuban Americans living in Miami, and more information on their comings and goings, than exists for their counterparts in other standard metropolitan statistical areas in the U.S.

Readers will notice that Chapter 5, on Cuban American culture, presents extensive data on pre-Castro Cuban society. I spent a significant amount of time evaluating the pros and cons of taking this course. After all, non-Cuban readers could interpret the approach as an attempt to glorify or at least idealize the social milieu that preceded the Cuban Revolution. Eventually, I decided to take that risk for two reasons. One, because of the enormous influence Cuban society had on the exiles materially, culturally, and psychologically. Moreover, religious and fraternal institutions such as the ones discussed in Chapter 6 played key roles before and after Castro, both in Cuba and in the U.S. I believe that unless this background is made part of the Cuban American experience in the U.S., the fast-track acculturation and entrepreneurial success of Cuban Americans of different generations could not be fully understood. Also, without mention of the influence of pre-Castro culture and society, the reader may wonder why Cuban youth born and raised in revolutionary Cuba—and fairly isolated from the outside world—expect a standard of living similar to what is found in many developed countries.

Likewise, a dearth of information about pre-Castro's material and non-material culture may leave unanswered questions about the entrepreneurial success and behaviors of the early exiles shown in Chapter 8. Also unexplained would be the socioeconomic adjustment of second-generation Cuban Americans to a competitive highly technological American society, a dynamic explored in Chapter 5.

Beyond these considerations, I believe it's important to summarize the historical information presented in Spanish-language publications but not previously available in English.

The Cuban government's propaganda has often succeeded in suppressing, recreating, and reinterpreting—at the expense of national and international audiences—events and facts about the island's pre-Castro history and society. An objective presentation of these facts enables readers in the U.S., Cuba, and elsewhere to recognize both the assets and liabilities of Cuban Americans as a group.

Hopefully, this book, among other media, will contribute in offering a balanced perspective on the Cuban American community for historians, academics, and stakeholders. The last chapter speculates on post-Castro scenarios in Cuba and the U.S. to help readers envision future events in U.S.-Cuba relations and their impact on Cuban Americans. Chapter 3 provides background for this speculation.

Readers may notice that the chronology shown in Appendix C places the beginnings of the Cuban Revolution in 1959. According to multiple sources, including Fidel Castro himself, the Cuban people would not have supported his guerilla warfare against Batista if he had revealed his revolutionary plans and beliefs. During the struggle against Batista by Castro and other clandestine groups, the revolution was understood by most in the context of past republican political movements, like the ones of previous decades that aimed at overthrowing the government to restore political order, promote social change through democratic institutions, or re-establish the nation's constitution.

The process of replacing Cuba's entire social and institutional order with alternative Marxist-inspired institutions began when Castro assumed power in 1959, and it was consolidated in the 1970s.

The metropolitan area popularly known as Miami is a jurisdiction officially named Miami-Dade County. Miami-Dade County encompasses several cities and areas such as the cities of Miami, Miami Beach, and Hialeah. Cuban Americans reside in all parts of Miami-Dade County. The latter is located just north of the Florida Keys.

I

LATINOS IN THE UNITED STATES

WHO IS LATINO?

Before the 1970 Census, most U.S. Hispanics defined themselves by their national ancestry. Similarly, a New Yorker might say "I'm Irish," or "I'm Italian," when asked, "What are you?" In the 1960s and earlier, Hispanics in the U.S. would identify themselves as Mexicans, Puerto Ricans, Cubans, etc. Many still do. But by the 1980s and beyond, the generic term Hispanic became popular for a variety of reasons—the government's use of the term in data reports, its adoption by corporate America, and the growing diversity of Hispanic nationalities among immigrants. The evolution of the terminology used for self-identification is complex. In the early twentieth century, Hispanic groups called themselves Latin American. And since the 1960s, Mexican Americans have split their preferences among the terms Mexican, Mexican American, Chicano, Californio, and others. Other nationalities use alternative names too, such as boricuas, puertoricans, or nuyoricans (Puerto Rico), nicas (Nicaraguans), cubiche (Cuban), etc. All of the above are used indistinctly depending on one's preference. Some individuals use labels that identify with a region, city, or state in the U.S., while others may choose labels irrespective of regional significance. And then there are the linguistic purists, philosophers, and historians who pull from their own discipline's lexicon, using such terms as Ibero-American, Latins, Spanish, etc. It is unlikely that all parties will agree upon a universal term to classify persons born in Latin America or Spain, or whose ancestors came to the U.S. from those countries. In this book, I use the terms Hispanic, Latino, and Hispanic American without intending to express a preference. Ultimately, I consider the choice personal and respect those of others.

PAST ROOTS AND TODAY'S PRESENCE

While sharing some common traits, U.S. Hispanics make up a diverse ethnic group. They are White, Black, Olive, and Mulatto. Some speak only Spanish, or English. Some are poor and live in central cities while others are wealthy and live in suburbia or upper-income neighborhoods. Some were born in the U.S., and some immigrated. The number of Hispanic Americans is growing fast, and Hispanics live everywhere in the U.S. The growth is reflected in the fact that 40 percent of all Hispanic Americans were born in America.

Although increasingly diverse as a group, most Hispanic Americans are intertwined by a common origin that extends as far back to the fifteenth century. In 1492, more than a century before the pilgrims landed at Plymouth Rock, Christopher Columbus, financed by Queen Isabella and King Ferdinand, sailed from Spain hoping to discover precious metals and spices in the Indies. Instead, he landed on a Caribbean island three months later. Henceforth, Spanish sailors, businessmen, and missionaries colonized vast territories in today's North, Central, and South America. They set in motion the histories, cultures, and national identities of what today constitutes Latin America, a conglomerate of nations and countries with a combined population of more than 400 million. Latin America has close land and sea borders with the U.S.

As an aggregate group, U.S. Latinos are among the five largest Latino populations in the world, eclipsing the populations of Canada and Spain. By 2002, close to 40 million Hispanics accounted for 14 percent of the U.S. population. They are the fastest growing group in the U.S. (almost 5 percent, or 10 million, in the last decade), and account for almost half of the growth of the U.S. population.

Hispanics have made an important contribution to American history since the days of the Continental Army. Nonetheless, their massive immigration, the growing presence of Latinos in government and the economy, and their current status as the largest minority group in the U.S. makes them a frequent focus of controversy in our national and international policy debates.

RESIDENTIAL EXPANSION AND PERCEPTION

Most Hispanic Americans (70 percent plus) are concentrated in five states of the Union, and three out of four Hispanics live in the West and the South.

Clearly, since the 1980s, the Latino presence in the U.S. has become salient in states where few Hispanics had previously lived. During the last decade, more than twenty states doubled their Latino population. Between the years 1990 and 2004, this growth was especially noticeable in states like Alabama, where Hispanics grew by almost 300 percent; Arkansas 500 percent; Delaware 204 percent; Georgia almost 300 percent; Kentucky 250 percent; Maryland 136 percent; North Carolina almost 600 percent; South Carolina 326 percent; Tennessee 410 percent; and Virginia 165 percent. In four of thirteen Atlantic-region states, Hispanics now account for 13-17 percent of the total population. In North Carolina, for example, the state's estimated 400,000–plus Latinos affected at least 5 percent of the state's economy.

Hispanics are also spreading throughout states with historical Hispanic settlements. In Palm Beach County, Florida, for instance, almost 20 percent of the population is Hispanic. And Palm Beach is not an isolated case. Hispanics in the state of Florida continue to grow in leaps and bounds. Between 1990 and 2000 alone, 70 percent of Florida counties experienced 100-200 percent growth in their Hispanic population. In 15 percent of counties, it grew by 200 percent or more.

By 2004, there were more Hispanics living in the state of Florida (3,304,832) than in the state of New York (3,076,697).

Notwithstanding this comparison, the Hispanic populations in New York State and New Jersey increased between 1990 and 2004. By 2004, approximately 1,250,000 Latinos lived in the Garden State.

Although Hispanics are moving into all spheres of American society, large numbers of the general public still perceive them as unfamiliar aliens of dubious benefit to the U.S. There seems to be a "disconnect" between the appreciation of contributions by the overall Hispanic community and appreciation of individual successes of entertainers like Gloria Estefan, Andy Garcia, and Jennifer Lopez; financial leaders like Roberto Goizueta; or Hispanics who are U.S. Cabinet members, governors, and members of Congress, like Bill Richardson, Henry Cisneros, Carlos Gutierrez, Mel Martinez, Bob Menendez, and Ken Salazar. The list of Hispanic members of Congress is much larger and grows every year.

Hispanic laborers from abroad are sought by thousands of non-Hispanic employers and households but rejected by legislators and ordinary citizens who fear Latinos, including children of immigrants, will taint the social fabric of America. Hardly a year passes when a Hispanic student is not punished for speaking Spanish inside a public high school, although fewer such instances occur over time.

Some Hispanics return to their countries of origin after accumulating savings in the U.S. Most stay here, legally or illegally, and while here remit a sizeable average of their earning (20–25 percent) to their families in the old country.

HISPANIC NATIONAL GROUPS

Before 1960, U.S. Latinos were almost entirely Mexican American and Puerto Rican. Following the advent of the Cuban Revolution in 1959 and subsequent armed conflicts in Central America, a new era of migration by Latinos into the U.S. began. Within a decade, Hispanic American nationalities grew to include Colombians, Nicaraguans, Salvadorians, Hondurans, Dominicans, Brazilians, and others. More recently, Venezuelans and Argentineans have joined the ranks of U.S. Hispanics.

By the year 2000, the U.S. Census reported that 66 percent of all U.S. Hispanics were Mexican American, 9 percent Puerto Rican, 4 percent Cuban, 14 percent from Central and South America, and 6 percent "Other Hispanic."

LANGUAGE AND NATIONAL ORIGIN

One evening, back in the days when I lived in New York City, I was a panelist at a PTA meeting at a Queens public high school discussing Aspira's Consent Decree. After our panel finished its presentation, a parent approached me and asked if "Hispanics from different countries spoke the same dialect." That day it struck me that one cannot assume most people will have any level of familiarity with Hispanic issues or with U.S. Latinos any more than most Hispanics are familiar with the intricacies of ethnic strife in the Balkans or the tribal social organization in Africa.

Now that I bring up this point, let me say that most Hispanics speak Spanish and, except for certain phrases, words, and idiosyncrasies, we understand each other. There are few exceptions in Latin America, like Brazilians who speak Portuguese and isolated monolingual Indian tribes who speak dialects like Aymara or Quechua.

Language predominance among U.S. Latinos is closely tied to place of birth, income, and occupation—the higher the income and educational level, the greater the tendency to be bilingual in English and Spanish, or English monolingual. Regardless of their national origin, most second-generation Hispanics and all third generation are bilingual or English dominant. There is no data that suggests Hispanic Americans don't learn English. Even a third of foreign-born Hispanics are English dominant or bilingual.

This fact notwithstanding, today's Hispanic Americans have a greater tendency to preserve some degree of Spanish than did European immigrants of the nineteenth and early twentieth century. The latter and their offspring adjusted to American life under a monolingual philosophy that had little regard for their native languages. Comparatively, today's Hispanics are not subjected to the same pressure faced by the former to assimilate and abandon the culture of the old country. Also gone are the sheer prohibitions and punishments faced by Spanish speakers in many states prior to the 1960s.

MIGRATION HISTORIES

Hispanic national groups came to the U.S. with different historical backgrounds. Some Mexican Americans have histories rooted in former Mexican territories before their occupation and absorption by the U.S.

Mexican Americans reside in the U.S. for a multitude of reasons. Some remained here as their lands became part of the U.S., others came from Mexico fleeing political upheaval, others arrived in search of a better life, and more recently a growing number of middle class professionals and entrepreneurs have moved to the U.S. seeking social stability and a better quality of life.

Puerto Ricans have been U.S. citizens since 1917, after experiencing almost two decades of U.S. occupation. The island became a U.S. Commonwealth following Spain's defeat in the Spanish–Cuban American War.

The first large immigrant wave of Puerto Rican islanders into the U.S. mainland took place in the 1950s. Until the 1980s and beyond, Puerto Ricans were concentrated in the Northeast—mostly New York City and in areas of New Jersey and Connecticut. In recent years, Puerto Ricans have migrated from the New York metropolitan area into hundreds of U.S. communities, where few if any Hispanics lived before.

During the 1970s, guerrilla warfare, civil wars, and political instability in Central America, coupled with U.S. involvement in these conflicts, brought hundreds of thousands of Guatemalans, Peruvians, Salvadorans, Nicaraguans, and others into the U.S. These groups settled for the most part in Florida, California, and New York.

Likewise, political and social instability and persistent poverty have brought large numbers of Colombians to the U.S. Their presence in New York City and Miami neighborhoods and their influence in media and business have been noticeable for the last three decades.

INCOME AND EDUCATIONAL TRENDS

Since the 1980s, the general trend for Hispanic Americans has been toward gradual socioeconomic improvement, yet they still rank low relative to the total U.S. population.

For instance, there are almost three times more Hispanic poor than the U.S. average (9 percent). Although there are more Hispanic homeowners than ever before (50 percent), the group remains well below the national average (67 percent).

Puerto Ricans show the highest poverty rates of the three largest Hispanic national groups. At 26 percent, they are three times poorer than the U.S. average and compare unfavorably with poverty rates for Central and South Americans (15 percent) and Mexican Americans (20 percent). On average, Puerto Rican households earn $5,000 less than Latino households.

The average Latino household income is $10,000 dollars below the average of all U.S. households. Nonetheless, 18 percent of all Hispanic households earn more than $50,000 annually, and there are about 1.5 million affluent Hispanic households in the U.S.

During the last decade, Hispanics as a whole improved their high school graduation levels (60 percent) but still lagged behind all other major racial and ethnic groups in the U.S., especially non-immigrant Whites. This educational gap varies by state. Between 1992 and 2005, Latino fourth and eighth graders in California, New York, Florida, and New Jersey closed the gap with White students in math and reading. But during the same period, the separation in math and reading between Latino and White fourth graders increased in Arizona and Colorado.

Still, by the year 2000, more than one in ten Hispanics nationwide held bachelors degrees, and well more than one-half million had obtained advanced degrees. Among the U.S. Hispanics showing notable educational progress are mainland Puerto Rican professionals, who have reached higher college graduation rates than Mexican Americans.

BOOMING ECONOMICS

Regardless of how they are perceived or their socioeconomic status, U.S. Hispanics constitute a major consumer group. By 2005, their buying power reached $700 billion and is expected to grow to $1 trillion by 2010. Hispanic-owned businesses have played a significant role in the group's social advancement, not unlike the role played by churches in African American communities.

By the turn of the century, there were more than 1 million Hispanic-owned businesses in the U.S. generating gross revenues in excess of $200 billion. Hispanic businesses account for almost 6 percent of all U.S. businesses and employ 1.5 million workers. During the last decade, Hispanic-owned firms grew by 30 percent following a 100 percent increase during the period 1982–92. Comparatively, Hispanic-owned businesses are growing four times faster than the average for all U.S. firms, and their receipts have doubled in the last ten years. On the whole, more than one third of all Latino-owned businesses were located in five U.S. metropolitan areas. Close to 40 percent of these firms were owned by Mexican Americans and were located in California and Texas. The rest of the businesses owned by U.S. Hispanics belonged to Cuban Americans, Puerto Ricans (6 percent), Spaniards (5 percent), and the rest by other Hispanics/Latinos.

For more than two decades, in addition to establishing their own businesses, Hispanic Americans have begun to hold managerial and executive jobs in Corporate America. Still, with the notable exceptions of a few top-level executives and senior managers in *Fortune* 500 corporations, Latinos are generally found in technical and mid-level professional positions, or in human resources departments, but seldom at the highest corporate levels.

The exceptional cases emerged in the 1990s, when a few major U.S. corporations brought in Latinos as CEOs, COOs, and directors.

LATINO POLITICS

The twenty-first century has put Latino politics on the nation's agenda. A recent presidential election (2000) was decided by a few hundred votes, the narrowest margin ever in U.S. history. Of the 270 electoral votes needed to win the presidential election, 213 are in the 10 states where the majority of U.S. Hispanics live, notably California, Texas, Florida, New York, and Illinois.

The number of Hispanic voters has grown significantly since several Hispanic organizations have begun conducting large voter-registration campaigns. For instance, the number of Hispanic voters in the 1996 and 2004 presidential elections grew from 5 million to about 7 million. By 2005, there were 9.3 million Hispanic Americans registered to vote nationwide.

U.S. Latinos are not seizing the political opportunity offered by a population in excess of 40 million. For instance, in the 2000 election, less than half of Hispanic eligible voters cast their ballots. Still, Latino-elected and appointed officials are becoming more ubiquitous in American communities. By 2004–05 there were about 4,500 Latino elected officials in thirty-eight states. They included 3 U.S. senators, 1 governor, 22 U.S. representatives, 200 state legislators, and some 4,200 elected officials at the county and municipal levels. In addition to elected officials, thousands of Hispanic American appointees serve at every level of government, from the federal executive branch to local advisory boards and commissions.

Despite the growing presence of Hispanics in government and a handful of high-level appointments, this group remains underrepresented in middle and senior levels of the federal government. Representation also lags in the largely non-Hispanic U.S. media.

In the early 1960s, the vast majority of U.S. Hispanics were registered in the Democratic Party. By the 1980s, Republicans had captured most of the Cuban American vote. By the 2004 election, the ratio of U.S. Hispanic Democrats to Republicans dropped to about 60–40 or 65–35, depending on estimates. The significant Latino presence in both U.S. political parties is bound to create new dynamics in the way our political leaders count the Latino vote and should open new doors to Latinos in American political spheres.

Occasionally, one hears the question of whether Cuban Americans—particularly those in Miami-Dade—are part of the Latino community or the rest of the U.S. The answer to that question is generally based on personal experiences or in brief, selected, and occasional media coverage of Cuban Americans mostly dealing with massive immigration, the embargo, or the latest anti-Castro initiatives.

The chapters that follow will help the readers not only to form their own opinions but also to learn other facts about Cuban Americans, their adjustment to U.S. life, and their relations with others, now and prospectively in the post-Castro era.

SOURCES AND SUGGESTED READINGS

Cuban American Policy Center, *Hispanic National Groups in Metropolitan Miami* (Miami: The Cuban American National Council, Inc., 1995).

Roger Díaz De Cosió, Graciela Orozco, and Esther González, *Los Mexicanos en Estados Unidos* (México: Sistemas Técnicos de Edición, 1997).

Hispanic Business 500 Directory (Hispanic Business, June 2004).

"Hispanic Growth Changing Face, Flavors of Florida," *The Miami Herald,* 8 October 2000.

Edward Iwate, "Immigrant Business Can Have Wide Economic Impact," *USA Today,* 16 November 2005.

"Land of Opportunities," *U.S. News and World Report,* 20 June 2005, p. 64.

Waldo Lopez-Aqueres, *An Overview of Latino-Owned Business in the 1990s* (Los Angeles: The Tomas Rivera Policy Institute, September 2000).

Alex Meneses Miyashita, "Latino Students Boost Scores, But Gaps Persist," *Hispanic Link Weekly Report,* Vol. 24, 9 January 2006.

Naleo Educational Fund, *National Directory of Latino Elected Officials* (Los Angeles, 2002).

"New Realities May Now Count in City Politics," *New York Newsday*, 22 February 1991.

A. Portes, ed., *The New Second Generation* (New York: Russell Sage Foundation, 1996).

A. Portes and R. L. Bach, *Latin Journey: Cuban and Mexican Immigrants in the United States* (Berkeley: University of California Press, 1985).

A. Portes and Richard Schauffler, *Language and the Second Generation* (Baltimore: The John Hopkins University Press, 1993).

Jorge Ramos, *The Latino Wave: How Hispanics Will Elect the Next American President* (New York: Harper Collins, 2004).

Fresia Cadavid Rodriguez, "Cuban Exiles Exert Most Foreign Policy Influence," *Hispanic Link Weekly Report*, 27 October 2003.

Christine Senteno, "Latino Experts Call for Congressional Hearings on Federal Employment Gap," *Hispanic Weekly Report*, Vol. 23, 19 December 2005.

U.S. Bureau of the Census, *Current Population Reports* (Washington, D.C.: Sample Survey, U.S. Department of Commerce, Bureau of the Census, March 1972).

U.S. Bureau of the Census, Hispanic 1997 (Washington, D.C.: 1997 Economic Census, Survey of Minority-owned Business Enterprises, Company Statistics Series, February 2001).

U.S. Small Business Administration, *Minorities in Business, 2001* (Washington, D.C.: Office of Advocacy, U.S. Small Business Administration, November 2001).

II

DEFINING CUBAN AMERICANS

There are several ways to define a Cuban American. In simple terms, Cuban Americans are persons born in Cuba who left the island and now live in the U.S.; they also comprise persons of Cuban ancestry born in the U.S. Beyond this generalization, some may reject a hyphenated identity and prefer to see themselves simply as Americans, or as Cubans, Latinos, or Hispanics, as the case may be. For the purpose of this book, I will refer to Cubans in the U.S. as Cuban Americans. My apologies to all who disagree with the use of this term. I hope they will understand the difficulty of finding a commonly accepted label.

Since 1970, U.S. Censuses, immigration studies, and other private market research have provided estimates for the number of Cuban Americans living in the U.S. The U.S. 2000 Census of Population and Housing counted the persons of Cuban descent at 1,241,685, or less than 1 percent of the total U.S. population, and about 4 percent of all U.S. Hispanics. By 2004, the count increased to more than 1.3 million. This figure represents a tenfold growth in the number of Cuban Americans living in the U.S. since Fidel Castro's rise to power in 1959. For the last four decades, Cuban Americans have been the third-largest national group among U.S. Hispanics.

Notwithstanding the frequent portrayal of Cuban Americans as a monolithic, recognizable group, this community has become more diverse since 1960. Just consider that by 2004, Cuban Americans with refugee status constituted a minority in relation to permanent Cuban American residents and citizens. Cuban Americans first came to the U.S. as tourists and soon turned into exiles/refugees. In time they became citizens, as new rafters and boaters from the island received the lesser status of entrants, then migrants, and eventually wet or dry footers, a distinction that determined whether the U.S. government allowed them to stay. The other one third of all Cuban Americans include people born in the U.S. who speak English most of the time—as American is their predominant culture—and take pride in the heritage and traditions passed on by their elders.

Cuban Americans have a large proportion of Spanish speakers, which results from successive immigration waves, a concentration of Cuban Americans in South Florida, and the strong sense of community felt by most Cuban Americans.

The majority of Cuban Americans are White (90 percent), but their features, whether Black or White, would make them hard to identify if they walked by or sat next to you in a public place, that is, unless they spoke in Spanish or in English with an accent you could discern as Cuban.

The date and mode of arrival (air or sea), birthplace, and place of residence in the U.S. are significantly related to the demographic characteristics and socioeconomic status of Cuban Americans. This is especially true for recent immigrants in their first ten years after arrival. Essentially, everything else being equal, Cuban Americans who live in states other than Florida likely will have higher incomes, more years of schooling, and a greater command of English. The economic, educational, and linguistic differences among Cuban Americans sharpen when comparing recent arrivals with U.S.-born and longtime residents.

Americans of Cuban descent have the highest income and educational levels of all Cuban Americans. These second-generation Cuban Americans have median incomes close or equal to the average of non-Hispanic White Americans. Most are high school graduates, and their proportion of college graduates comes close to the average of the U.S. population as a whole.

The adjustment pattern of Cubans arriving in four large refugee waves (e.g., 1959–62, 1965–72, 1980, and 1994) reveals similarities, although the perception by American public opinion has differed substantially over the years.

Since the nineteenth century, Cuba's geopolitics and socio-economic development have been inseparable from the United States. Hence, it was no surprise when most Cubans escaping Castro's Cuba sought refuge in the U.S. and were accepted in large numbers by every American president since Dwight D. Eisenhower.

III

CENTURIES-OLD CUBAN AMERICAN RELATIONS

Centuries-old relations between Cubans and Americans have made the U.S. a safe refuge and friendly destination for Cubans, especially during periods of war and political turmoil on the island.

Cuba, the largest and most strategically located Caribbean island of the Antilles, is narrow and six hundred miles long—about the size of Pennsylvania. Located ninety miles away from Key West, it has a population of more than 11 million. It was discovered by Christopher Columbus in 1492 and ruled by Spain until she lost the Spanish-Cuban American War in 1898.

A U.S. military governor ruled the island as a protectorate between 1898 and 1902, the year when the first Cuban president, a former Cuban American teacher in New York, was elected to rule. Cuba then became a republic under the Platt Amendment, a U.S.-imposed amendment to the Cuban constitution giving the U.S. the right to intervene in Cuban affairs to protect American interests. With President Franklin D. Roosevelt's support, the Platt Amendment was repealed in 1934, and Cuba went through a period of civilian and military rulers, of presidents freely elected, endorsed by the U.S., or forcibly imposed on Cuba by Cubans themselves. Then, in 1958, an insurrection opposing the Batista government gained control of the island, and Batista and his closest followers fled Cuba that New Year's Eve. A week later, Fidel Castro, whose revolutionary movement had led guerrilla warfare for two years from Cuba's eastern-most mountains, entered Havana and soon positioned himself as the nation's leader. His ascent to power marked the beginning of the radical social change of Cuban

21

society known as the Cuban Revolution.

To date, the radical transformation of Cuban institutions, the abolition of civil society, the elimination of private property, and the silencing of all opposing voices have divided Cuban society and left emigration as one of the few available choices to those who disagree with the government and/or seek freedom and a better life.

The critical events in Cuba's modern political life triggered the largest exodus of Cuban nationals in the island's history. But they alone do not explain why Cubans chose to flee to the U.S. instead of other countries, or why the U.S. accepted several waves of them as refugees, asylees, or migrants. A brief review of the relations between Americans and Cubans may shed light on this issue.

COLONIAL PERIOD

From the early colonial period of the 1500s, Cuba's location at the mouth of the Gulf of Mexico made the country a key port of call for traffic between Europe and America. For two centuries, Spain's fleet and other maritime convoys gathered in Havana—sometimes in the hundreds—on their return voyage to the Old World. Cuba was also the seed of church and government for Spain's newly conquered territories, what is today Central America, South America, and, yes, Florida. In those days, maritime traffic and commerce in Cuba came hand in hand with regular access to cultural life in Spain, its metropolis, and brought to Havana not only merchants and sailors but artists, musicians, academics, and elites from all over Europe.

By the late eighteenth century, Cuba had developed an educated elite of Creoles (Cuban-born descendants of Spaniards) who began to advocate, or conspire, for a change in the island's colonial status to autonomous or independent. From that time to the early days of the republic, groups of Cuban patriots and intellectuals favored the island's annexation by the U.S. But neither the majority of Cubans living on the island nor those abroad have favored such a scenario.

In 1762, Cuba's academic and intellectual development was enhanced by a one-year military occupation of Havana by an English fleet. The island's wealth grew as a result of free commerce on the island and eventually free trading between Cuba and the British North American colonies. At the time, more people lived in Havana than in New York, Philadelphia, or Boston.

The historical roots between Cuba and the U.S. also extend to the Americans' own fight for independence. By 1781, England had captured Charleston and had a strong military presence in Georgia and South Carolina. General Washington was desperate for money to continue waging military operations. The Count de Saint Simon, an officer in the French expeditionary force sent to support the American colonists in their War of Independence, sailed from what is today the Dominican Republic, reached Havana, and contacted Cuban-born Governor Juan Manuel Cajigal. The latter immediately helped raise funds for the American revolutionary army. Many in Havana assisted in this effort, but none like a group of Creole women who donated jewels and diamonds with an estimated value exceeding one million British pounds. In addition, Havana played an important role as a center of naval operations for military actions, including one that resulted in the continental army's capture of Pensacola, Florida, from the British.

By the eighteenth century, Cuba published its own newspapers and was influenced by the modern thinking of intellectuals like A. Caballero and Felix Varela, who shared John Locke's philosophy on representative government, individual rights, and free trade. Arguably, the influence of these and other Creoles on Cuba's social and intellectual development helped Cubans to share in the great social experiment beginning in North America in 1776.

THE CENTRAL ROLE OF FLORIDA

For more than geographic reasons, Cuba has played a significant role in Florida's history as far back as the seventeenth century, before a Cuban national identity was forged in the island.

The first Cuban-born governor of Spanish Florida was Laureano Torres de Ayala, a well-educated Creole who presided over the completion of San Marcos Fort in today's St. Augustine, Florida.

Governor Torres de Ayala was followed by Juan de Ayala, also Cuban born. Raised in a modest family, he arrived in Florida as an infantry private and ended up governing the territory for two years. Even shorter was the time in office of the next Cuban-born governor of Florida, Manuel Jose de Justiz, one of five interim governors between 1700 and 1763.

The last Cuban-born governor of Florida was Colonel Jose Cappinger, who in 1821 presided over the military change of command from the Spanish army to a U.S. army contingent under Colonel Robert Butler. Two years earlier, Florida had been ceded to the U.S. under a treaty signed by Spain's minister Juan de Onis and U.S. secretary of state John Quincy Adams.

Cuba produced more than just eventual American political leaders. One example is Bishop Luis Peñalver y Cardenas, the first Catholic bishop of territories extending from Florida to Quebec. Born in Havana, Cuba, he occupied the Episcopal seat of Florida and Louisiana in 1793.

U.S. INFLUENCE DURING CUBA'S WAR OF INDEPENDENCE

Later in the nineteen century (1885), in the interim period between Cuba's two wars of independence, Cuban American Fernando Figueredo represented the Florida State Assembly during the thirteenth session of the legislature in Tallahassee. Figueredo, a naturalized American of Cuban origin and an army colonel who helped lead Cuba's liberation from Spain, also served as superintendent of schools in Monroe County, Key West, and later as Mayor of West Tampa, both in Florida.

Cuba's proximity to the U.S.—social, geographic, and otherwise—has been a major determinant of today's Cuban American experience. For example, back in 1837, while still Spain's colony, Cuba operated the first railroad in the Americas, years before Spain did. Between Cuba's first war of independence and the late 1890s, tens of thousands of Cubans, including war patriots, migrated to the U.S. for temporary and sometimes permanent stays. These Cubans founded cigar factories, patriotic clubs in support of the war, and mutualist societies—in Tampa and Key West, as well as in New York City, where Cuban priest and philosopher Rev. Felix Varela founded the city's first hospital for the indigent. In the same city, Cuban Patriot and intellectual Jose Marti wrote numerous articles and essays for American newspapers during his stay.

New York City is of special significance to Cuban Americans; it was the city where Cuba's flag flew for the first time ever. The flag was designed by Miguel Teurbe Tolon in 1849 at a guest house on Warren Street in lower Manhattan.

By the late nineteenth century, more than 5,000 Cubans (15 percent Black) had a sizeable presence in West Tampa and in Key West, where most inhabitants were Cuban until 1894. At the time, most Black Cubans worked in factories alongside Whites, while others acted as labor organizers and operated small businesses, which included a boarding house, a bar and restaurant, a warehouse, and a barbershop. Some of them founded an Afro-Cuban newspaper, and others became leaders of Cuba's pro-independence party (PRC).

Moved by strong nationalist sentiments and decades of exile and war against Spain, many Cubans questioned the timing of U.S. intervention in Cuba's war of independence (1898) and its Platt Amendment sequel (1902). Still, the fact remains that the U.S. fought against Spain, organized elections soon afterward, and eventually eliminated the Platt Amendment.

Moreover, Americans helped Cuba rebuild after two decades of war. With the economy and infrastructure devastated, Cubans suffered from poor public health and sanitation. According to the United Nations 1959 Statistical Book, Cuba's mortality rate per 1,000 inhabitants ranked the lowest in Latin America. The writings of John Dewey strongly influenced Cuba's public educational system and pedagogy with a marked lay scientific orientation; and after World War I, in the early years of Cuba's Republican era, Americans worked alongside Cuban intellectuals like Antonio Sanchez de

Bustamante to develop democratic institutions and to formulate international labor laws.

CUBA'S REPUBLICAN YEARS

The first president of Cuba was D. Tomas Estrada Palma, a naturalized U.S. citizen elected in absentia. For more than a decade before assuming the presidency, he lived in Central Valley, New York, where he taught Spanish and history and became headmaster of his own school.

Throughout Cuba's Republican era, relations between Cuba and the U.S. were important, particularly for the island's governance and for its tourism and sugar industries. During these pre-Castro years of the republic, Cuba's national currency, the peso, was traded at par with U.S. dollars. During World War II, the Cuban naval forces in coordination with the U.S. Navy sank two German submarines operating in or near Cuban waters. Many other Cubans joined the U.S. armed forces to fight overseas. During the Big War and later during the Korean conflict, Cuba was a steady supplier of sugar and minerals to the U.S. In both conflicts, several Cuban doctors, one of them a practitioner in Miami until his death in 2005, served as active officers in the U.S. medical corps. By the late 1950s, Cuba's strong economy was largely owned by Cubans and received annual boosters of preferential prices and quotas by the U.S. for the island's sugar industry.

Prior to Castro's revolution, Cuba's per capita income ranked among the first three in Latin America, was almost as high as Italy's and exceeded Japan's. Also, 1 in every 39 Cubans owned an automobile, a high ratio compared to Mexico's 1 in 91 and Brazil's 1 in 158.

In 1958, Cuba ranked second in Latin America in the number of physicians per capita (64,231) and third in the proportion of dentists. In that year, Cuba spent a greater proportion of its national budget on education than any of its Latin American counterparts.

By the 1950s, Cuban society was influenced by the U.S. more

than any other country in Latin America. Cuba was the first country outside the U.S. to broadcast a World Series baseball game (on the island's national television station), and served as an inspiration for American literary masterpieces, such as *The Old Man and the Sea* by Ernest Hemingway. It also created the genre of Cuban jazz, appreciated by legends like Dizzie Gillespie and familiar around the world. Innumerable American artists such as Tony Bennet, Robert Merrill, Nat King Cole, Frank Sinatra, Billy Daniels, Cab Calloway, Dorothy Dandridge, and others performed in Havana, were seen or heard in hotels and nightclubs, or could be enjoyed on Cuban radio and TV before 1959. And, as far back as 1920, Cuba had its professional baseball league, where stars like Babe Ruth played. Prior to the revolution, U.S.–Cuba relations helped put the island's cultural and entertainment world on par with that of developed countries of comparative size. By 1950, Cuba had about 400 movie theatres—the largest one holding more seats than Radio City Music Hall—and scores of nightclubs, such as the renowned Tropicana.

In the 1950s, one of every five Cubans owned a radio, one in twenty had a TV set, and 145 AM and FM radio stations broadcast throughout the island. Cuba also boasted 10,000 jukeboxes, two magazines with a national circulation of 320,000, and a ballet company featuring one of the American Ballet Theatre (ABT) founding dancers, Alicia Alonso.

Cuba's first symphony orchestra was founded as early as 1908, just six years after Cuba became a republic. Shortly after, bel canto idols like Caruso, Gigli, Puerto Rican Paoli, and Schipa would perform before Cuban audiences. Eventually, this cultural tradition continued with appearances of worldwide idols like Tebaldi, Victoria de los Angeles, and scores of others.

American influence in pre-revolutionary Cuba, particularly in Havana, reached most spheres of life and was noticeable in dress fashions, food (hot dogs, burgers, milkshakes, etc.), and music. Also, commonly used English terms such as "parquear" (from park), consumer items like cigarettes, not to mention items as varied as hairstyles, late-model automobiles, and medical and dental equipment appeared as manifestations of the U.S. role in Cuba's development during its republican years.

Here in the States, Cuban-born performer Desi Arnaz pioneered TV studio filming techniques and is still seen on reruns of the "I Love Lucy" series. And world-famous pianist and composer Ernesto Lecuona became the first Latin American nominated for an Oscar in 1942 with his song "Always in My Heart." In today's U.S., there are seven towns named Cuba; they exist in Alabama, Illinois, Kansas, Missouri, New Mexico, New York, and Ohio (Havana also can be found in several states, most notably Florida).

Most likely, the influence of American culture reached Cuba before most of the world. Given these and countless other examples of the long-term relationship between the American and Cuban people, it is understandable that anti-Castro Cubans looked to the U.S. for help in opposing Castro, and as a refuge when Castro's plans for Cuba's future became evident.

CASTRO'S REVOLUTION AND MASSIVE EXODUS

Events ushering the first wave of Cubans into exile included the confiscation of privately owned properties by Castro's government and the nationalization of U.S. businesses. These first revolutionary expropriations affected U.S. businesses and large Cuban land holdings. Confiscations soon spread to industry and urban properties, then to medium-size, and eventually small businesses. The assertion of government control of all of Cuban society included the banning of private professional practices (medical, dental, etc.), the takeover of private schools, and the seizure of Cuba's organized labor.

The new revolutionary government conceived and permitted traditional civil institutions only if they served the revolution. The separation of powers (executive, legislative, and judicial) was consolidated and subsumed under single-party, military rule that controlled government, culture, and the economy.

The regime, supported by the army and security forces allegedly on behalf of the Cuban working class, stripped the media—radio, newspapers, TV, and magazines—of independence and absorbed it as part of the government's information and propaganda apparatus. As the government took over all sectors of the Cuban economy and society, it proclaimed itself Marxist-Leninist. Opposition to the revolution's control of Cuban society, and especially to Fidel Castro's leadership, was met harshly. At first, members of Batista's military, then Catholic leaders, political and business leaders, professionals, and thousands of others received long prison sentences or death by firing squads. Some just disappeared or died under unknown circumstances. Shortly after 1959, opposition to Castro's revolution included some of his own top-ranking officers from his rebel army, as well as civilian members of Cuba's revolutionary government. All failed in their efforts to change the course and leadership of the revolution. By 1960-61, tens of thousands realized that values such as freedom of speech, movement, religious vocation, and independent press were not options in Castro's Cuba. For them, little could be done to change the situation, unless the United States could help topple Castro.

Between the years 1959 and 1962, more than 250,000 Cubans arrived in the U.S. It doubled the number of Cubans living in the U.S. in 1960.

For these hundreds of thousands of Cubans, the U.S. offered the only outlet for escape. It was the only country in the world where Cubans could emigrate with their families. Often, parents sent their children unaccompanied to the U.S. under the care of the Catholic Church and thousands of American foster families.

Between 1959 and 1962, as Cubans fled the island in large numbers, critical events affected U.S.-Cuba relations. These relations deteriorated almost daily and were formally suspended in 1960.

THE BAY OF PIGS INVASION

During the first three years of the revolutionary takeover, tens of thousands of Cubans came to the U.S. with different types of visas and were allowed to stay indefinitely. Nevertheless, most of them were hopeful, if not certain, of a prompt return to a free Cuba.

By April 1961, the U.S. had recruited, trained, equipped, and directed a volunteer expeditionary force of about 2,000 Cubans in the U.S. The objective—to invade Cuba and overthrow the Castro regime with the support of the Cuban people. The Brigade 2506 soldiers were mostly Whites commanded by a Cuban Black officer. They included other Blacks and Mulattoes, Cubans of several religious persuasions and social strata, former members of Batista's army as well as Castro's Rebel Army, and a mix of professionals, blue-collar workers, and students. Most of them were young, averaging twenty-three years, and their military experience ranged from seasoned (former military and naval pilots who had graduated from U.S. military academies) to minimal or nonexistent (students, pilots, boat owners, water sports enthusiasts, and youngsters with no previous military skills or background). While overwhelmingly Cuban, the brigade included volunteers from Argentina, Puerto Rico, and the U.S. For almost nine months, the group was trained by the U.S. Central Intelligence Agency (CIA) and other U.S. military personnel in general warfare in Guatemala, Nicaragua, Puerto Rico, Panama, and the U.S. The mission, eventually known as the Bay of Pigs invasion was authorized by both Republican President Dwight D. Eisenhower and Democratic President John F. Kennedy. Planned to take place on April 17, 1961, it aimed to destroy Castro's air force with surprise air attacks for two days and then give close air support to an invading force of some 1,500 men. On the eve of the invasion, as the expeditionary force and U.S. supporting personnel totaling 3,000 landed on Cuba's beaches in the Bay of Pigs and set to engage 75,000 Castro's troops, President Kennedy ordered a stop to all air operations.

Without the planned air support, Castro's small air force put a halt to the invasion by sinking several transport and supply ships and preventing the advance of the landing force beyond the landing sites. After several days of fighting in the mangroves, cut from any further U.S. military support and without coordination with the anti-Castro resistance, 114 men were killed and 1,200 brigade soldiers were forced to surrender and were later imprisoned. After being captured, a group of them was placed inside a sealed truck and died of asphyxiation during transportation by the Cuban military. According to U.S. government-classified information available to the general public in 2005, CIA officials knew the invasion would fail without support from the U.S. military. The absence of this support, along with a poor choice of landing sites, an insufficient invading force, and minimum coordination with underground groups opposing Castro inside Cuba precipitated failure less than three days after the expeditionary force landed on Playa Giron and Playa Larga.

In 1963, most brigade prisoners were freed and returned to the U.S. through the payment of ransom totaling $53 million in food and medicine. The U.S. government met the demand with assistance from the American Red Cross, the Kennedy family, and a Cuban American Families Committee.

After the Bay of Pigs invasion, regular passenger flights between Cuba and the U.S. came to a halt, setting the scenario for successive migratory waves from Cuba to the U.S. By 1962, the U.S. and the Soviet Union were already involved in a cold war that would last for decades. In October of that year, U.S. naval forces intercepted Soviet ships bringing nuclear warheads to a secret missile base in Cuba. After negotiations between the two countries, the Soviet Union ordered its ships back, and the U.S. agreed not to invade Cuba. It also agreed to prevent others from invading Cuba from U.S. territories.

GROWING PERMANENT ROOTS DURING THE COLD WAR

The political events confronting the U.S. with Cuba and the Soviet Union, and the massive exodus of Cubans from the island, made it even more likely for the U.S. to accept large numbers of anti-Castro Cubans into the U.S. It showed the world how the Cuban people voted with their feet against the Sovietization of Cuba. After 1962, the migration of Cuban Americans became part of U.S. foreign policy, while Cuba's government used it as a scapegoat for popular discontent and growing scarcity. In the U.S., Cuban exiles were first a showcase of the failure of communism, then a pervasive legislative issue. Cuban exiles eventually became a large concentrated voting bloc with an unyielding interest in U.S. foreign policy and a strong ethnic identity.

By the late 1960s, Cubans in the U.S. had realized that a prompt return to Cuba was not around the corner. While anti-Castro efforts continued in different ways, hundreds of thousands of Cuban Americans began to plant their roots in the U.S. with the help of several U.S. government agencies. By November 1966, Public Law 89-732, signed by President Lyndon Johnson, allowed Cubans paroled into the U.S. to apply for a change of status to permanent resident without the previous requirement of having to leave the U.S. territory. The visa fee requirement was also waived. Furthermore, Cubans could claim up to thirty months of their previous stay in the U.S. as parolees as part of their five-year eligibility requirement for U.S. citizenship.

To this day the Cuban Adjustment Act still helps Cubans remain in the U.S. and normalize their status one year after arrival. Earlier, the Cuban Refugee Program had helped hundreds of thousands of Cuban Americans adjust to life in the U.S. and pursue the American dream. Also, in the early 1960s, the Pedro Pan (Peter Pan) Project brought fourteen thousand unaccompanied Cuban minors to the U.S. Families sent children to the U.S. under the care of the Catholic Church. These families often made the decision in light of the Cuban government's increasing control of educational institutions and of the life of children and students.

Relations between Cuba and U.S. have existed for three centuries, even when both countries were colonies of Spain and England, respectively. They have been friendly and binding for the most part. If the past serves as prologue, historical ties between both countries will be re-established in the post-Castro era.

SOURCES AND SUGGESTED READINGS

Rafael D. Arango, *Mi Pequeña Historia de Cuba* (Miami: Colonial Press Internacional Inc., 2000).

José Agustín Balseiro ed., *Presencia Hispánica en la Florida, Ayer y Hoy 1513-1976, Durante la Revolución de las 13 Colonias* (Miami: Hispanic Studies Collection, Ediciones Universal, 1976).

Nestor Carbonell y Rivero, *Elogio del Coronel Fernando Figueredo Socarras* (La Habana, Cuba: Imprenta El Siglo XX, 1935).

Teachers College Press, *Dewey on Education* (New York: Teachers College, Columbia University, 1959).

Theodore Draper, La Revolución de Castro, *Mitos y Realidades, Segunda Edición* (México: Congreso Por la Libertad de la Cultura, 1962).

"La Libertad, Homenaje Al Pensamiento Democrático En Cuba," *El Nuevo Herald,* 20 de mayo 2003, Suplemento Especial.

Enrique Fernandez, "New Orleáns: Latin Culture Runs Deep in the Crescent City," *The Miami Herald,* 7 September 2005.

Margarita Garcia, *The Development and Maintenance of a Myth: Unsupported Assertions that Tomas Estrada Palma was a Converted Quaker; Paper Presented at the Ffiteenth Biennial Conference of Quaker Historians and Archivists* (Newberg, Oreg.: George Fox University, 2004).

Susan D. Greenbaum, *Afro-Cubans in Ybor City* (Gainesville: University Press of Florida, 1986).

Susan D. Greenbaum, *More Than Black: Afro-Cubans in Tampa* (Gainesville: University Press of Florida, 2002).

Interview with Maria Rubio and Wilfredo Allen (Miami, 30 September 2005).

J. Isern, *Gobernadores Cubanos de la Florida* (Miami, 1999).

Peter Katel, "A Relationship Gone Adrift" *Poder* (September 2003).

Jeff Koenreich, John B. Donovan, and Pablo Perez-Cisneros Barreto, "After Bay of Pigs" (Miami: Unpublished Manuscript, 2004).

Levi Marrero, *Un País en Desarrollo: Cuba En La Década de 1950* (Miami: Edición de la Junta Patriotica Cubana, 1990).

Carlos Alberto Montaner, "Cuba y U.S.A: Como La Geografia Define La Historia," (author correspondence, 9 December 2004).

Marifeli Perez-Stable, *The Cuban Revolution, Origins, Course and Legacy* (New York: Oxford University Press, 1993).

"Revista Hispano Cubana," *Primavera* (Madrid, España: mayo-julio 1998).

Gerardo Reyes, "La Guerra que Posada Carriles No Pudo Ganarle a Fidel Castro" *El Nuevo Herald,* 15 de mayo del 2005.

Fresia Cadavid Rodriguez, "Cuban Exiles Exert Most Foreign Policy

Influence," *Hispanic Link Weekly Report,* 27 October 2003.

Armando Salas-Amaro, José Marti, *Maestro Masón: Antonio Maceo, Hombre o Titán* (Miami: September 2004).

State of Florida, Senate Journal, *A Journal of the Proceedings of the Senate of the State of Florida at the Thirteenth Session of the Legislature* (Tallahassee: 6 January 1885).

Jaime Suchlicki, *Historical Dictionary of Cuba* (London: The Scarecrow Press Inc., 1988).

U.S. Department of State, *Chronology of Cuban Affairs, 1958-1998* (Washington, D.C.: Bureau of Inter-American Affairs, 12 January 1998).

La Voz Católica, *Nuestro Primer Obispo: Don Luís Peñalver y Cárdenas* (Miami: mayo del 2005).

IV

UNDERSTANDING MIGRATORY WAVES

Cuban migration to the U.S. reflects both the island's state of affairs and U.S.-Cuba relations. Extensive Cuban immigration to the U.S. dates back one and a half centuries. Motivated by the turmoil and devastation of Cuba's wars of independence (1868-78 and 1895-98), Spain's military conscription policies, or political leanings, tens of thousands of Cubans left the island and settled primarily in New York, Tampa, Key West, and New Orleans.

Recent Cuban migration to the U.S. is associated with escape from the island. Means of transportation is a significant predictor of the Cuban émigré's profile. This specially applies to the first two major exile waves that arrived by air in the U.S. between 1959–62 (250,000) and 1965–72 (300,000). The two other waves arrived here by sea, one in 1980 (125,000) and the other one in 1994 (30,000). Cubans who flew into the U.S. in the 1960s were quickly granted asylum, perceived as refugees or exiles. Conversely, Cubans who came in large, unplanned maritime waves in 1980 and 1994 were labeled either as "marielitos," a diminutive of "mariel" (their Cuban port of departure) or as "balseros" (rafters), named after the makeshift boats used to cross the Straits of Florida. The general public perceived both as undesirable aliens or illegal economic migrants. Furthermore, the first air-transported waves received benefits afforded by the U.S. government such as refugee status, visa waivers, the Cuban refugee program, and the Cuban Adjustment Act. By contrast, the U.S. government classified maritime arrivals as entrants, migrants, and more recently, dry- or wet-feet migrants, a status distinction that determined whether migrants could stay in the U.S. or whether coast guard vessels would return them immediately to Cuba.

In addition to the four major migratory waves, post-Castro Cuban arrivals fit into four other groups. Of these smaller groups, two have been flown into the U.S.–a group of Cuban political prisoners with their families in 1979 (10,000), and several thousand Cubans who left the island at different times and reached the U.S. via third countries such as Mexico, Spain, and Jamaica.

One of the two remaining smaller groups was a maritime flotilla of 5,000 Cubans picked up by their U.S. relatives–at Castro's invitation–at the Cuban port of Camarioca in 1965. The other maritime wave of Cuban émigrés consisted of small scattered groups of rafters who escaped the Castro regime in boats and rafts, especially during periods when living conditions in Cuba suffered sharp decline and the prospects of leaving for the U.S. were minimal. While the exodus of these "balseros" occurred in streams of small groups, the combined total has surpassed 70,000 since 1959.

These migratory waves and their reasons for leaving require further discussion to understand.

LARGE MIGRATORY WAVES

EARLY EXILES (1959-1962)

As a group, the first wave of Cuban émigrés comprised the best educated. Almost 40 percent were high school graduates and about the same percentage fell under the categories of professionals, managers, and business owners.

The exiles of the early 1960s came almost entirely from Cuba's capital, Havana. They over-represented Cuba's White population as well as the country's upper strata in the 1950s. In just two decades after their arrival, these early refugees and their offspring played salient roles in business, academic, political, and artistic spheres, not only within the Cuban American community but also in mainstream America. They made up the only large group of Cubans allowed by the government to leave the island with their relatives without facing restrictions of age, sex, or occupation.

Of all the groups, Cuban exiles of the early 1960s most reflected pre-revolutionary Cuban culture. They brought memories of their school years and professional training at Cuban universities when courses in Marxism-Leninism were not required. Admitted as parolees-refugees, they nonetheless identified themselves as exiles. They became de-facto guardians and historians of traditional Cuban pre-revolutionary culture.

The exodus of so many Cubans who served as leaders in Cuba's civil society had significant international ramifications. It gave the U.S. an opportunity to showcase negative aspects of Marxism and the Soviet system. The American public generally welcomed these leaders, and the U.S. government granted them parole status with indefinite voluntary departure, as well as assistance from the U.S. government through the federally financed Cuban Refugee Program.

FREEDOM FLIGHTS (1965–1972)

The next large wave of airlifted Cubans came as a result of a 1965 memorandum of understanding between Cuba and the U.S. It was larger than the previous wave, which had settled in the U.S. by 1962, but it excluded, at the Cuban government's mandate, political prisoners, males eligible for military service aged fifteen to twenty-six years, and technicians and skilled personnel.

These restrictions, coupled with the previous departure of many members of the upper strata, affected the profile of Freedom Flights passengers coming to the States between 1965 and 1972. Also, airlift preferences were given to U.S.-related unmarried children under the age of twenty-one, to the parents of unmarried children underage, to spouses, and to underage brothers and sisters. Because of the restrictions, the Freedom Flights/Airlift arrivals over-represented students, children, and housewives and included a comparatively lower percentage of professionals and entrepreneurs, not to mention a lower average of years of schooling.

MARIEL BOATLIFT (1980)

In 1978, at Fidel Castro's invitation, a group of some one hundred Cuban Americans met with Cuban government officials in Havana. Subsequently (1979–80), the Cuban government allowed about 100,000 Cuban Americans to visit the island, an unprecedented move widely criticized by both the Cuban exile community and many in Cuba's communist circles. Suddenly, exiles previously called "worms" or "lumpen" by communist officials were labeled "the community abroad" or "the Community." Many Cuban communist cadres found this shift in perception difficult to digest. The change also confounded and disturbed Cuban exile groups active in anti-Castro politics.

And just a year later, a series of incidents unfolded in Havana. In April 1980, a group of would-be exiles commandeered a public transit bus, crashed the front gate of the Peruvian Embassy, and forced their way into the embassy grounds. Driven perhaps by the success of Cuba's international military forays in the 1960s and 1970s and by his perceived inroads with a sector of the exile community, Castro again invited all who wanted to leave Cuba to do so. Within two days, 10,000 Cubans entered the Peruvian Embassy grounds, and many more headed that way from all over the island. Realizing the embarrassment this episode would cause him, particularly in Latin America, and being a consummate counter-puncher, Castro invited Cuban American exiles to come for their relatives at the Cuban Port of Mariel. Cuban exiles responded once again to Castro's invitation, and the Mariel boatlift began, redirecting world attention away from the incident's Latin American context and reframing it as part of the Cuba–U.S. conflict.

During five months in 1980, the largest wave of seafaring Cubans left the island aboard approximately 2,011 large and small vessels, privately owned by Americans, mostly from South Florida, en route to the U.S. The arrivals included a mix of a few thousand political prisoners and other dissidents rounded up by Cuban security forces. Another few thousand included common criminals, several hundred Jehovah's Witnesses, homosexuals, and relatives of

Cubans already in the U.S. The group included mostly male, single adults with a larger proportion—compared to previous waves—of Blacks, Mulattoes, and blue-collar workers.

On average, marielitos had fewer years of schooling, engaged in a wider variety of blue-collar occupations, and included fewer professionals than groups that had left in previous years.

GUANTANAMO RAFTERS/BALSEROS (1994)

More than a decade later, and again prompted by the Cuban government's encouragement, 30,000 rafters and boaters headed north, mostly from the coastal areas of Havana's metropolitan area, seeking to reach the U.S. By then, Castro had been in power for forty years, the Soviet bloc had collapsed, and the compassion-fatigued American public had little tolerance for massive immigration. Also, the potential benefits to U.S. foreign policy were not as clear as they had been in 1962, when the first wave of Cuban upper- and middle-strata political refugees reached the U.S.

As in the previous Mariel flotilla, the rafter migration traced to a combination of Cuba–U.S. relations and to events inside Cuba. After the Mariel exodus, opportunities for Cubans to come to the U.S. continued to diminish, because not many Cubans qualified under the U.S. visa standards. By 1993, thousands were fleeing the island solo or in small groups on rafts and small boats. Then, on March 13, 1994, a Cuban military vessel rammed and sank a tugboat carrying dozens of Cuban citizens escaping to the U.S. Thirty-nine passengers, including men, women, and children, drowned, thrown overboard by the impact or by the force of the gunship's water cannon. Barely a month later, thousands of Cubans gathered in Havana's "malecon" seawall neighborhood to watch government agents stop a ferry manned by Cubans fleeing the island. The crowd became enraged and began throwing stones at the glass windows of neighborhood stores and at Cuba's police officers. Police and military reinforcements, including government "storm troopers" (Brigadas de Respuesta Rapida), quashed the riot. Days later, Fidel Castro withdrew frontier guard units and announced that all who wanted to leave the island could do so. This marked the third time—counting the flotillas of Mariel and Camarioca—that Castro opened the gates of migration to allay internal pressure, create a potential burden to the U.S., and shift the world's attention away from protests inside Cuba. In an almost festive mood filmed by the international media, thousands of Cubans carried small rafts made of drums, lawnmower engines, tires, etc. through the streets of Havana. They headed for nearby beaches and coastal areas and sailed due north into the Straits of Florida. The U.S. Coast Guard intercepted hundreds of rafters, and President Bill Clinton ordered them interned in our naval base in Guantanamo, Cuba, where they remained for about one year before being admitted to the U.S.

Decisions on the admittance of émigrés were again based upon the wet-feet/dry-feet classifications applied to undocumented Cubans; the latter could stay, but the former had to return. The event altogether resulted in the granting of additional U.S. visas to Cubans wanting to emigrate to the U.S., per the agreement reached between Cuba and the U.S. Another consequence of the agreement—Cuba resumed its practice of restricting escape from the island.

Possibly, rafters ("balseros") constituted the most diverse group of Cuban American émigrés ever. They included a mix of children and elderly, Black and White, teachers and other professionals, health workers, manual laborers, unemployed youth, scientists, and members of Cuba's military. Cuban rafters interned in Guantanamo—more than past defectors—represented different geographic areas in Cuba. They included a large number of high school graduates but just a few individuals proficient in English.

MIGRATORY FLOODS AND STREAMS (1959–2005)

In addition to the four large migratory waves already mentioned—two aero-transported and two having arrived in large and small boats—thousands of Cuban émigrés have reached the U.S. at other times.

CAMARIOCA BOATERS (1965)

The first small maritime wave of Cubans sailed to the U.S. in 1965, just three years after regular commercial flights between Cuba and the U.S. were suspended. For three years, Cubans who wanted to leave the island lacked the means to do it. This period challenged Fidel Castro's leadership, as he faced increasing criticism from Soviet-backed Cuban communist party leader Anibal Escalante and guerrilla groups fighting in Cuba's central mountain ranges. Castro had differences with former comrades about the functioning of the Cuban economy, and the appearance of early signs of food shortages would haunt the Cuban population for decades to come. Thus, in 1965, Fidel Castro, seizing an opportunity to provide an escape valve to the disaffected and to shift the perception of Cuba's internal problems by attributing them to the conflict with the U.S., invited all Cubans who wanted to leave the island to be picked up by their U.S. friends and relatives at the Cuban port of Camarioca.

Within two months, 3,000 Cubans reached the U.S. and received asylum. Although smaller in scale than past waves, the Camarioca event marked the first instance of unplanned maritime Cuban migration to the U.S. promoted by the Cuban government. It was also the first instance of the Cuban government using illegal immigration as a weapon to open negotiations with the U.S.

INDIVIDUAL RAFTERS (1959-2005)

In recent times, smaller groups of Cuban citizens have been leaving Cuba in small boats and homemade rafts, especially during the 1966-79 and 1981-94 periods, when leaving Cuba through normal migratory channels proved most difficult. Estimates suggest that 63,000 rafters have reached the U.S. alive, while 16,000 others have perished in the waters of the Straits of Florida.

AIRBORNE, THIRD-COUNTRY ARRIVALS (1959–2005)

Since the advent of the Cuban Revolution, thousands of Cuban individuals and families have left the country by air with visas from third countries, such as Spain, Mexico, and Venezuela, and later established residence in the U.S. as circumstances permitted.

AIRBORNE, CUBA–U.S. VISA ARRIVALS (1995–2005)

After the 1994 U.S. Coast Guard interception of balseros and their interment in the U.S. naval base in Guantanamo, Cuba, the U.S. and Cuban governments reached a migratory agreement. It mandated that Cubans who escaped the island without documentation had to return if apprehended before setting foot on U.S. soil; escapees that managed one step on that soil could stay. As part of the agreement, the U.S. granted Cuba a minimum of 20,000 visas per year, either through regular immigration quotas, humanitarian channels, or a lottery popularly known in Cuba as "el bombo." Since 1995, about 200,000 Cubans have entered the U.S. legally on regular flights between the two countries. By the late nineties, when the visa lottery started, more than half a million Cubans had applied to leave the island. Cuba then stopped granting additional lottery visas despite U.S. support for this orderly process.

THE FUNCTIONS OF MIGRATION

Fidel Castro has consistently used Cuban émigrés as pawns to create migratory crises for the U.S. and to portray the failure of the Cuban Revolution as the result of a conflict between the two countries. Additionally, Castro has used immigration waves as an escape valve for releasing the pressures and challenges posed by fellow revolutionaries (Escalante, Matos, and Sori Marin) and by discontented Cubans.

For the U.S., the first waves of Cuban immigration provided a valuable showcase of failed tropical communism during the Cold

War era. The U.S. also received thousands of trained, experienced physicians and other professionals pursuing freedom and the American dream. Attempts to reach the U.S. in small seafaring crafts have cost the lives of 16,000 rafters, drowned or eaten by sharks in the Straits of Florida. Fortunately for several other thousands of Cubans, immigration has meant the difference between freedom and political imprisonment or death by firing squad.

For most exiles, life in the U.S. has provided unique economic opportunities. To all, exiles and immigrants, America has provided the individual and social freedoms lacking in Cuba, a country departed often with feelings of sadness and hope accompanied by memories and traditions that linger deep in the hearts of the Cuban American community.

SOURCES AND SUGGESTED READINGS

Holly Ackerman, *An Analysis and Demographic Profile of Cuban Balseros, 1991-1994* (Coral Gables, Fla.: Issue Paper, 1995).

Pablo Alfonso, "Camarioca: Cuatro Décadas de Éxodo y Dolor," *El Nuevo Herald,* 25 de septiembre del 2005.

Efrén Córdova, ed., *40 Años de Revolución: El Legado de Castro* (Miami: Ediciones Universal, 1999).

Antonio Jorge, Jaime Suchlicki, and Adolfo Leyva de Varona, *Cuban Exiles in Florida: Their Presence and Contribution* (Miami: Graduate School of International Studies, University of Miami, 1991).

The Legislative Link, Vol. III, Issue 1 (The United Way of Florida Inc., 6 November 1992).

Mirta Ojito, *Finding Mañana: A Memoir of a Cuban Exodus* (New York: The Penguin Press, 2005).

A. Portes and A. Stepick, *City on the Edge: The Transformation of Miami* (Berkeley: University of California Press, 1993).

A. Portes and Richard Schauffler, *Language and the Second Generation* (Baltimore: The John Hopkins University Press, 1993).

Lisandro Perez, "Immigrant Economic Adustment and Family Organization: The Cuban Success Story Reexamined," *International Migration Review,* Vol. XX, No. 1 (Miami: Florida International University, 1986).

V

CULTURE

If culture is understood as learned, shared behavior that one acquires as a member of society, then social environments, of past and present, have influenced the cultural traits of Cuban Americans. For Cuban Americans there are three significant milieus, namely pre-Castro culture in Cuba, U.S. culture, and post-Castro culture in Cuba. Also, because culture evolves, time of arrival in the U.S. is a key determinant of cultural variations within the Cuban American community.

EARLY EXILES AND PRE-CASTRO CULTURE

The first Cuban refugees of the 1960s laid the foundation of today's Cuban American culture. These exiles were raised as adults and young adults in pre-Castro Cuban society. They studied curricula offered by the public and private schools and universities of a large, mostly urban educational system. The free enterprise society and civil institutions strongly influenced Cuban education, laden with norms and mores, real and ideal, and reflecting deeply rooted nationalistic feelings, Judeo-Christian values, a strong liberal intellectual tradition, and a lay vision of society. Cuba's intellectual and educational foundations are rooted in Spanish-Creole history, French revolutionary ideals and jurisprudence, and Cuba's historical ties with the U.S.

In the early days of the republic, Cuba began developing a system of public and private educational institutions that trained most of the upper- and middle-class exiles of the early 1960s.

By 1958, Cuba's population was roughly 6 million. There were 21 public high schools throughout the island with a combined enrollment of 30,000 students. In addition, Cuba had 245 Catholic, 60 Protestant, 4 Hebrew, and 467 private lay schools, most of them in Havana.

Almost 20,000 students were enrolled in public universities in three provincial capitals—Havana, Santa Clara, and Santiago. Five private universities claimed a combined student population exceeding 2,000, and more than 150,000 students were enrolled in some 3,000 vocational, business, and technical schools.

Most of the first Cuban exiles resided in Havana and to a lesser extent in urban areas in the island's six provinces, which reflected the social, economic, and educational imbalance in pre-Castro Cuba. During the last pre-Castro years, there was a four to one illiteracy ratio between rural and urban Cuba. This further explains why the vast majority of the first immigrant wave to the U.S. consisted of middle- and upper-class Havana residents.

Middle- and upper-class Cubans brought with them heavy baggage, not so much in the form of material objects or wealth but in prescriptions and memories of a well-developed culture and institutions. As they settled in the U.S., they revived the daily Spanish and "Cubanisms" of their times ("se la comió," "apaga y vamonos," "está de bala," "paragüero," etc.); the religious and patriotic celebrations (Christmas Eve dinner and Independence Day); Cuba's rich musical traditions (cha, cha, cha: boleros); business practices (entrepreneurship); national heroes (Marti, Maceo); and ideal role models and symbols (liborio, güayabera shirts).

The social, economic, and political upheaval caused by Castro motivated the flight of early exiles from Cuba. Despite their diverse pre-Castro partisan politics, almost all shared strong anti-Castro and/or anti-communist beliefs, and they favored the U.S. democratic and economic systems.

SUCCESSFUL CULTURAL PLURALISM

In their adjustment to American society, Cuban Americans have adopted key aspects of the American way of life, while preserving and re-creating many customs and institutions from pre-Castro Cuba. Data from as far back as 1980–87 shows that over half of south Florida Latinos—a majority of them Cuban Americans—could speak some English, despite the fact that almost one of every three of the area's Hispanics was a senior citizen or was a recent arrival to the U.S. College and high school graduation rates support the Cuban Americans' ability to speak English. (For U.S.-born Cuban Americans, English is their primary language, and available studies show they are well adjusted and contribute significantly to American society. These second-generation Cuban Americans, a third of all Cuban Americans, already outnumber the exiles of the early 1960s.)

Cuban Americans display several indicators of cultural pluralism in their successful adjustment to American society. Studies show that Cuban American students in the Miami area feel less discriminated against than other ethnic students, have high educational aspirations, and prefer English despite possessing varying degrees of proficiency with Spanish. A Cuban American friend of mine recently summarized this collective self-confidence by noting that "we never doubted we would succeed." Additional aspects of the Cuban American successful integration into American culture and society are the socioeconomic and educational successes of second-generation Cuban Americans (predominantly English speakers), the high naturalization rate of Cuban immigrants, the high proportion of Cuban Americans who are registered voters and turn out to vote, the wealth generated by the more than 100,000 Cuban American–owned businesses, and the salutary role Cuban Americans play in helping newcomers as employers of first resort. More than a dozen Cuban Americans have played prominent roles as top executives in *Fortune* 500 companies. Their roles require behaviors, idiosyncrasies, and lifestyles typical of American culture and mostly absent in traditional, pre-Castro business culture and relations. In 2004–05, the second Cuban American CEO of a *Fortune* 500 corporation, Carlos Gutierrez, was appointed as U.S. Secretary of Commerce. He followed the steps of another Cuban American, Roberto Goizueta, one of the most successful CEOs of Coca-Cola. Among the thousands of Cuban Americans in public service, there are cabinet and sub-level appointees, several generals and colonels of U.S. Armed Forces, the chair of the U.S. Nuclear Regulatory Commission, and the 2005 president-elect of the American Psychiatric Association. Since 1980, seven Cuban Americans have served as U.S. ambassador to several countries and international bodies, and three have served as presidents of American universities. Cuban Americans also boast nationally known artists and entertainers like Andy Garcia, Gloria Estefan, Cameron Diaz, and Pulitzer Prize winner Nilo Cruz.

As they become acculturated, Cuban Americans of first and second generations are notable patrons of the arts, not only in Miami-Dade but also in cities like Palm Beach, New York, Atlanta, Chicago, and Los Angeles. In Miami, they play salient leadership roles as donors, event organizers, board members, and volunteers in philanthropic community-wide institutions such as the Orange Bowl Committee, the Miami Grand Prix, Chambers of Commerce, Center for the Performing Arts, the Miami City Ballet, the United Way, the International Miami Film Festival, and the Miami Book Fair. They also play such prominent roles in county museums, universities, hospitals, and international art festivals.

ACCULTURATION PROCESS

For Cuban Americans, adapting to American culture has involved interpreting rather than denying traditional Cuban culture. During the late 1970s and the 1980s, pre-Castro traditional rites of passage such as "Sweet Fifteen" parties began to take a more "Cuban American" character, as celebrants descended on swings to the dance floor or were carried on by young men dressed in traditional African/Mesopotamic costumes. Professional Cuban American choreographers often ran and directed the productions. For Cuban Americans, preserving Cuban culture, whether one personally experienced it or not, includes a remarkable number of events that exceed merely celebrating a traditional Christmas Eve dinner, eating guava pastries or black beans, smoking cigars, drinking a "cortadito" (Cuban coffee with a touch of milk), playing dominoes, or dancing Cuban salsa.

As an example, Cuban Americans in Miami have established one of the largest, if not the largest, university-based collections of Cuban and Cuban American archives and publications outside Cuba. Also, Cuban American businessmen have organized an annual exposition called "Cuba Nostalgia," where visitors buy CDs of Cuban music, step on a giant rug map of Havana to pinpoint their origin, view enlarged old photos of Havana's former upscale department store, and buy yearbooks (from Cuba's pre-Castro private schools), artifacts, paintings, and thousands of memorabilia items from the old country. On an even larger scale, Cuban Americans have organized "Calle Ocho" (Eighth Street), America's largest street festival, drawing upwards of one million people.

There is plenty of folklore in Miami. Recently, I personally experienced that Miami may be the only place on earth where you can play tennis without an advanced reservation or a wait, across the street from a cemetery, while listening to loud Afro-Cuban "bembé" music coming from inside the duplex apartment next to the court.

Today, a visitor to historical Cuban American neighborhoods—Miami's Little Havana and most of the City of Hialeah—can buy peanuts from a traditional street vendor (manisero) or fresh vegetables from a moving truck (a modern version of Cuba's "viandero").

Linguistically, Cuban Americans increasingly use Spanglish—words that blend English and Spanish but don't exist in either language—such as "friquiar" (freakout) and "frizar" (freeze). Another common tendency is the mixing of English and Spanish words within one or several sentences ("pon el heater").

The fact that Cuban Americans frequently speak Spanish relates to their concentration—60 percent of all Cuban Americans live in South Florida—to the consistent influx of new immigrants, to the large number of other Spanish-speaking immigrants in the area, to the education level of first-generation Cubans, and to the existence of bilingual-bicultural social institutions in Cuban American enclaves.

The "early exiles" of the 1960s and the Cuban immigrants who followed them have adopted other Cuban American customs unrelated to Cuba's traditional culture. It is hard to find a Cuban American home that does not observe Thanksgiving (usually with an added touch of rice and black beans) or does not partake in America's Independence Day celebration. Naturally, Cuban American workers take Labor Day off in September instead of May 1, Cuba's Labor Day. And to many Cuban Americans who came to the U.S. in the 1960s or later, names like John F. Kennedy, Ronald Reagan, or Henry Kissinger are more familiar than some Cuban presidents or ministers of the pre-Castro era, e.g., Machado, Aleman, and Hevia.

THE IMPACT OF MEDIA AND ENVIRONMENT ON DIVERSITY

While Cuban American culture is fundamentally shared by most Cuban Americans, it is not expressed or experienced uniformly. Instead, the customs, institutions, and demographics of their respective residential communities shape their cultural behaviors. The best example is the role that media plays in informing and occupying the attention of Cuban Americans. Miami-Dade's Spanish media broadcasts—radio broadcasts, in particular—provide hours of daily coverage of Cuba-related news events. About 60 percent of Miami-Dade Cubans listen to Spanish radio programs, and more than 55 percent read mainly Spanish-language newspapers. The information presented includes commentary and analysis of happenings on the island, family messages sent to relatives in Cuba, live telephone interviews with political dissidents, activities conducted by exile organizations, and news in the U.S. and worldwide related to Cuba. Recently, a Miami academic-professional gathering celebrating the launch of a book by a Cuban American economist was teleconferenced live to Cuban dissidents in Havana.

Miami-Dade radio stations' regular programming features editorials, forums, and roundtables on Cuba's history, especially its political history going back to the days of the republic. In Miami, a listener scanning AM radio stations is likely to hear the words Cuba or Castro within a matter of minutes.

Additionally, Miami Spanish radio stations play large roles as community information banks and as keepers of traditional culture. They maintain fading musical genres like the "decima guajira" (country music), host radiothons for a number of philanthropic-humanitarian causes, and broadcast health, medical, and financial advice talk-shows, not to mention advertisements for and debates on municipal politics and other ballot issues.

To a lesser degree, Miami TV stations broadcasting in Spanish and Spanish-language daily newspapers provide wide coverage of Cuba-related news and events. Even English-language local media in Miami offers more news about Cuba than the national TV networks and daily newspapers in other major cities.

In general, Miami-Dade viewers, readers, and listeners of Cuban news tend to be older Cuban Americans or recent arrivals whose primary language is Spanish. Yet the influence of media on Cuban Americans and Miami-Dade's socio-cultural life is, at the very least, perceived as important. The coverage of Cuban American politicians, exile leaders, community activists, and non-Hispanic political candidates in Miami-Dade's Spanish media attests to this.

Cuban culture permeates Miami-Dade in other ways. Cuban American organizations, political or otherwise, celebrate historical events unknown to or forgotten by most Cuban Americans. Also, dozens if not hundreds of restaurants and cafeterias located throughout the county feature traditional Cuban cuisine on their menus. Cuban music is played daily on radio and TV stations and is available on recordings sold at numerous music stores.

Place of residence accounts for differences among Cuban Americans. Cuban Americans living in Miami or in other cities differ, for instance, in their socio-economic status, the frequency of their interaction, the number of Cuban American cultural events they celebrate, the proportion of their friends and co-workers who are Cuban American, things such as the time their meals are taken, and the language of their preferred media. Moreover, demographics such as intermarriage rates are higher for Cuban Americans who live in California or Puerto Rico than they are for Miami Cubans. In fact, the cultural adaptation of Cubans to a commonwealth society like Puerto Rico with a familiar Hispanic culture and traditions, language, and geography results in the adoption of Puerto Rican residential and cultural patterns. These patterns differ from those found among Cuban Americans in cities like Miami, New York, and Los Angeles.

Cultural givens for Cuban Americans in Miami and Union City-West New York are less pervasive in cities like New York, Los Angeles, and Chicago, where two of every five Cuban Americans live. The absence of these givens combined with more ethnically diverse worksites and residential neighborhoods make experiencing Cuban American culture less frequent and comprehensive. Cuban Americans living in these large cities are more likely to read, watch, and listen to non-Cuban events covered by national TV networks and major U.S. newspapers.

Beyond Miami-Dade, media coverage of Cuba-related issues is minimal. The contrast exacerbates an informational and perceptual divide between the Cuban American community in Miami-Dade and the rest of the U.S. The evidence appears in the political arena. For instance, based on the local Miami environment, Cuban American groups may conduct media or public events in a fashion they perceive as beneficial to their anti-Castro efforts. However, most Americans perceive these events, when reported by national media outlets, as negative or different from what Cuban American groups had intended. Conversely, limited or inaccurate information on the Cuban Revolutionary process and the Cuban exile community may cause non-Cubans to perceive actions or statements by Cuban Americans as parochial and outside of America's mainstream.

THE CUBAN AMERICAN IDENTITY

Two different articles published by the *Miami Herald* and the *Chicago Tribune* showed the Cuban Americans' strong sense of identity on issues as varied as a child's destiny (remaining in the U.S. or being sent back to Cuba) and pet selection. In the article in the latter publication, a Cuban American conveyed her feelings on the Elian Gonzalez saga by saying, "Truthfully, during the Elian fiasco, we just got a surge of [Cuban] patriotism. . . ." In another article, another Cuban American felt the need to express her cubannes in her pet selection: "When I punched into an Internet search everything I wanted, it came up with Havanese. This was the only Cuban dog we could find. And we found a breeder close to Tampa." In the article, the breeder in question stated, "The Havanese Heyday was the 18th and 19th centuries; they were the dogs of the Cuban aristocracy. Cubans called them Maltese. . . ."

After reading the article, I couldn't help thinking that this happy "Cuban" dog owner was an isolated example readymade for the media, that is, until months later when I told the story to a Cuban American friend from California who readily interjected, "Oh, I have a Havanese dog too."

Roasting a pig on "Noche Buena" (Christmas Eve) or other special occasions was a tradition in pre-Castro Cuba. People practiced the custom in backyards, the countryside, or other open spaces. Those who didn't roast the whole pig roasted a leg in the oven or fried pork chunks. Trimmings consisted of yucca (cassava), white rice and black beans, perhaps tostones (fried yellow plantains), and a salad that included lettuce and "rabanitos" (radishes). This Christmas Eve meal was so popular among all social classes that it became a sub-theme of one of Cuba's most popular danzones (an autochthonus Cuban rhythm), La Mora.

Enter Miami Cuban Americans who have found contemporary ways of preserving and adopting the tradition. Pigs are now roasted inside a Cuban American innovation, "la caja china" (tin or wooden box), or purchased in whole or by the pound from restaurants, meat stores, and supermarkets. This centuries-old custom is widely celebrated by Cuban Americans, not only in Miami but throughout the U.S., as Cuban American families have found ways of bringing tradition into the twenty-first century. Recently, a Miami family with relatives living in a large Midwest city packed an uncooked pig on ice, checked it on their scheduled flight, and roasted it the next day in their relatives' backyard. Upon leaving Miami, their luggage, of course, included black bean grains and green bananas, which made their celebration feel genuinely Cuban. This is by no means an isolated story. Affluent Miami Cuban Americans are known to fly out pigs for their Christmas holiday celebrations to far away resorts such as Aspen and Vail, Colorado. On an even larger scale, "pastelitos" (pastries filled with guava and/or cheese), homemade desserts, mangoes from the backyard, and other "Cuban" delicacies are regularly shipped or carried by Cuban Americans from Miami to grateful friends and relatives who reside outside Florida. Not long ago, I took part in the same practice when I boarded commercial flights to visit my daughter, who had moved to North Carolina. On two separate trips my carry-on luggage included well-packed frozen servings of homemade black beans—Cuban style—and "ropa vieja" (shredded beef boiled and sautéd). Needless to say, my welcome to Wake Forest was especially warm.

For Cuban Americans "being Cuban" or "ser cubano" is quite personal and defined in different ways. For most, their identity is a source of pride linking Cuban Americans by a pervasive common culture and institutional bonds that transcend racial, religious, and generational factors.

Humor is one of the deep-rooted traits found in both Cuban Americans and Cubans in the island. From the pre-Castro era to the present time, Cuban writers and intellectuals have regarded humor as an essential trait of the Cuban personality. A Cuban American academic described the archetypical Cuban as one who joked about serious matters while taking jokes seriously.

For decades, Miami-Dade theaters in Cuban American neighborhoods have staged comic plays that mock and involve impersonations of Fidel Castro and other revolutionary leaders. In those plays and stand-up comedy routines, human and political themes of a truly painful nature to Cuban Americans but presented comically draw the laughter of a Cuban audience, seniors especially. Similarly, Cubans on the island exchange scores of street jokes and humorous tales about the harsh living conditions and arbitrary policies imposed by Castro's revolution.

Forging an identity has not been much of an issue for most Cuban Americans. Over the years, they have managed to blend traditional Cuban and American cultures in non-exclusive ways that allow them to become proud Americans. They still savor memories of yesterday's Cuba or, for second-generation Cuban Americans and their offspring, imagine an island they have never seen.

BLACK AND CHINESE CUBAN AMERICANS

The Cuban, or Cuban American, cultural identity cannot be fully explained without mentioning the formative roles of Afro-Cubans and Chinese Cubans, both in Cuba's culture and in the migration of Cubans into the U.S.

BLACK CUBAN AMERICANS

Afro-Cubans or Cuban Blacks, as they are called by Cubans (before and after the revolution), came to Cuba as slaves less than a century after Columbus discovered the island. Their influence on Cuban culture stems from four main factors.

1. The colonizing Spaniard males had encounters with African women that often ended in marriage—or permanent unions—or in the public acknowledgment of their offspring. In fact, the population growth of Blacks and Mulattoes influenced the political ideologies and actions of White Cuban Creoles, who feared a Black-dominated Cuban society.

2. Unlike other European colonizers, the Spaniards, Portuguese, and French kept African slave families together. Their Christianizing of African Blacks involved the pairing of Catholic saints with

African gods from Nigeria, the Congo, Angola, and East Africa, where most Cuban slaves had originated. The best known of the polytheistic practices that emerged is the Yoruba's Santeria and its Ifá cult, which believed that several deities represented gods and goddesses of the waters, war, roads, etc. Also present but less influential were the African cults of the abacuas, or Carabalís, the araràs, and Palo Monte, or mayombe.

3. The cross-pollination or cultural syncretism of Afro-Cuban cultural elements with the European cultural traditions shaped the island's creole culture as early as the eighteenth century. This syncretism resulted in the strong influence of African rhythms in Cuban music, and in the practice or validation of the Afro-Cuban Santeria (cult of the saints) religion by many Cuban Whites from all social strata.

4. The participation of Cuban Blacks in Cuba's wars of independence also factored in. The second-highest–ranking military officer in these wars was a Cuban Mulatto, Lt. Gen. Antonio Maceo. Incidentally, the Cuban Independence Army Commander-in-Chief was not a Cuban but a Dominican, Generalissimo Maximo Gomez. Gen. Maceo was not an isolated example of a high-ranking Black officer in Cuba's liberation army. After gaining the freedom granted by Cuban patriots during Cuba's first war of independence (1868–78), many Cuban Blacks joined Cuba's liberation army and moved up the ranks by distinguishing themselves in battle.

Given this background, it is not surprising that, despite their relatively small numbers in the U.S., Black Cuban Americans are inseparable from post-Castro Cuban American culture. For several reasons, Black Cuban Americans emigrated to the U.S. later and in smaller proportions than other social groups. The revolution promised early to improve their social and economic situation, and it provided reminders of abuses committed in the U.S. against Blacks. Also, the early Cuban émigrés were claimed by their relatives already in the U.S.—mostly upper- and middle-class Whites. In addition, the revolutionary government denied exit visas to Blacks more than to Whites to show the international community that Cuban Blacks supported the revolution and did not flee Cuba. Nonetheless, the proportion of Black Cuban Americans has increased over the years from less than 5 percent in the early 1960s to almost 10 percent by the turn of the century. Black Cubans are more present in massive maritime flotillas, group defections of musicians and athletes, and in spectacular escapes from the island as rafters, stowaways, hidden in wooden boxes shipped via air parcel to the U.S. from the Bahamas, and among passengers of automobiles converted into amphibian vehicles in Cuba's clandestine garage workshops. Despite their small numbers, several Black Cuban Americans have held leadership positions, civilian and military: in the failed Bay of Pigs invasion in 1961, as priests and ministers of Cuban American congregations, as artists and intellectuals, and as leaders of Cuban American associations from the 1960s to the present.

In Miami, most Black Cuban Americans live in neighborhoods with a significant Cuban American or Latino presence. They also live in areas like northern New Jersey or Manhattan. There are exceptions though, like in Central Florida, where a number of Black Cuban Americans have established a residential cluster hosting Afro-Cuban religious practices, with traits of the traditional "cabildo," or mutual aid society of yesteryear. Cuban American priests or Babalaos formed the church of "Babalu Aye" in Hialeah (Miami-Dade County), and more recently, Santeria practitioners have published full-page ads in the *Miami Herald* asking for the fair treatment of church members who wish to travel to Cuba for religious reasons.

Traditionally, believing in or practicing Santeria has not prevented Black Cuban Americans—or Whites for that matter—from being baptized or from considering themselves Christians or Masons, or both. For the most part, Black Cuban Americans marry other Cubans or Latinos, identify themselves as Black Cuban Americans, and often work with other Latinos in both government and private businesses.

The Black Cuban Americans who believe in or practice Santeria keep abreast of religious events in Cuba, Africa, and the U.S. Following traditions that date back to the nineteenth century, when Cuban religious followers knew the whereabouts of African Princes and Babalaos, contemporary believers in the U.S. keep track of happenings in Cuba and know when Cuba's Santeria priests visit. Cuban American Santeros, their church members, and other believers not only hold traditional religious ceremonies, consultations, and offerings, they also observe religious customs. For instance, during the first days of each year, Cuban American Babalaos in the U.S. (as in Cuba) make divinations or interpretations of what the year will bring in blessings, catastrophes, health, and wealth. Miami's newspapers and Spanish-language radio stations frequently discuss "La Letra," as this tradition is known.

The U.S. political party preferences of Black Cuban Americans either resemble the preferences of other Cuban Americans or at least show no sign of being institutionally different. Also, their adjustment to different Cuban American communities and institutions vary in ways similar to White Cuban Americans.

The inclusion of Cuban American Blacks as part of the Cuban community, geographically and institutionally, has not occurred seamlessly. Racial prejudices existed in pre-Castro Cuba, exist today, and no evidence shows that they have disappeared as part of the Cuban American experience. Feelings of marginalization, nourished by their relatively small proportion of the Cuban American population, exist among some Cuban American Blacks. Nonetheless, Black Cubans continue to leave the island in growing numbers as part of the Cuban Diaspora in the U.S.

CHINESE CUBAN AMERICANS

The hyphenated term Cuban-Chinese can be traced to the mid-nineteenth century, when Spanish colonizers started bringing groups of Chinese laborers to Cuba. Although they represented a small proportion of Cuba's population at the time, Cuban-Chinese distinguished themselves as soldiers and officers in Cuba's liberation armies during the country's two wars of independence. The largest of these Chinese migratory waves arrived to the island during the second decade of the twentieth century, bringing the Cuban-Chinese island population to about 50,000. By 1959, the Cuban-Chinese community numbered in the tens of thousands.

With a large concentration in Havana, Cuban-Chinese were notoriously hard workers and successful small-business owners. By the arrival of the Cuban Revolution, there were dozens of Chinese restaurants and "fondas" (popular low-priced eateries), newspapers, laundries, movie theaters, a bookstore, a cemetery, a bank, and countless street vendors. Cuban-Chinese also formed several fraternal and mutual aid associations, and a Chinese Chamber of Commerce. Chinese Cubans, as they were popularly known (chino-cubano), belonged to different Christian churches or held traditional Chinese religious beliefs such as Confucianism.

Most Chinese immigrants in Cuba, particularly the first waves, consisted of single males who formed families with Cuban Black, Mulatto, and White women.

The vast majority of Cuban-Chinese left Cuba during the first years of the revolution and settled in either Cuban American or Chinese American communities like Miami, San Francisco, or New York. Once in the U.S., many Cuban American Chinese established ties with both Cuban Americans and Chinese Americans.

Following the trend of other Cuban American groups, many of the offspring of this first generation of Chinese Cuban Americans appear uninterested in owning or managing small family businesses like restaurants and laundries. They show more of an orientation for professional and technical careers. By 2004, just a handful of Cuban-Chinese–American restaurants stood in New York City and Miami. And, not surprisingly, most of these restaurants offered American, Japanese, and other ethnic foods, in addition to the traditional Cuban-Chinese menu.

YOUNGER CUBAN AMERICANS AND RECENT ARRIVALS

In this century, the children and grandchildren of the "early exiles" of the 1960s are U.S.-born citizens. Their cultural equation is the reverse of their parents, and English is overwhelmingly their primary language. Their Spanish is often limited, and when conversations get difficult they typically revert to English. Still, communicating in Spanish is an expression of their Cuban roots, a source of pride for most. As much as they might enjoy dancing salsa, American music is their native music, and they know American history much better than Cuban history, pre- or post-Castro. As a group, they are better off financially than their parents and have few reasons to live permanently in post-Castro Cuba. For second-generation Cuban Americans, being Cuban does not mean longing for yesterday's nights in Tropicana or swimming at Varadero beach. Most have never been there, but feelings about Cuba and the attachment to things Cuban remain strong, even if derived from their elders' stories and histories as well as their upbringing around things Cuban. In some cases though, identity may become a more complex issue for second-generation Cuban Americans. It is not easy to identify second-generation Cubans in large U.S. cities like New York. Some may enumerate themselves in the census only as White or Black, and most speak English predominantly. The majority, now dispersed throughout the city's many neighborhoods, rarely attend Cuban American events.

For younger, more recently arrived Cuban Americans, information on pre-Castro culture was acquired (if at all) from older relatives in Cuba in relatively informal ways. During their years of schooling and as young adults, they belonged to youth groups such as "pioneros" (pioneers) or communist youth ("UJC"), instead of boy and girl scouts. While in school and through the government-controlled media, they received messages stressing that legitimate philosophy and history began and ended with Marxism; the motherland (patria) was inseparable from "the party" (communist) and the revolution. Both were inseparable from and unthinkable without Fidel Castro. Christmas was officially banned for decades until the Pope's visit in the late nineties, when Cuba also stopped being a constitutionally atheist country.

Despite the Cuban government's efforts to change the island's traditions, islanders continue celebrating, albeit discreetly, several of Cuba's cultural traditions such as Christmas Eve and Three Magi Day (Reyes Magos). Other events such as sweet fifteen parties and weddings are still celebrated openly but in accordance with government specifications—quotas for party cakes, refreshments, etc. In addition to the traditional Cuban rhythms still being played in today's Cuba, younger Cubans grew up to the tunes of revolutionary artists and songs not well known by older first-generation exiles or their offspring. Despite having grown up in socialist Cuba, recent arrivals adapt fairly quickly to the U.S. and to Cuban American culture. On average, it takes them less than a decade to integrate into Cuban American social life and culture. Cuban Americans who open their doors for recent arrivals help facilitate their adjustment.

The adaptation of recent Cuban arrivals to life in the U.S. and integration into the Cuban American community may be happening faster than one might expect. In 1994, I was the U.S. Ombudsman, or Civilian Liaison, in our naval base in Guantanamo, Cuba. For months, I had the opportunity to talk at length with hundreds of Cuban balseros (rafters) interned at the base camps. This large group of escapees from the island (30,000) consisted of Black and White men and women from different age groups and educational levels. Interestingly, these Cubans, most of them born and/or raised in revolutionary Cuba, had no problems in communicating (in Spanish) with Cuban Americans working on or visiting the base.

One evening, as I addressed a group of about one thousand in an October 10 patriotic celebration in one of the base camps, I witnessed how Cuban internees showed their love for their native Cuba. Notwithstanding their deep emotions toward the country they had just left, these Cubans hoped to start a new life in the U.S. I couldn't help thinking about the similarities in the feelings and expectations of these Cubans and of other Cuban Americans who had lived in the U.S. for decades.

HANDS ACROSS THE FLORIDA STRAITS

Excluding times of migratory flow, contact between Cuban Americans in the U.S. and Cubans on the island in the 1960s and 1970s occurred through letters and telephone calls among family members, or adversarially through military encounters and anti-Cuban government operations. Periods of minimal contact precipitated low levels of reciprocal interest between Cuban islanders and Cuban Americans in their respective cultural developments.

Around the late 1970s, and certainly after the Mariel boatlift of 1980, Cubans in the U.S. and on the island increased their contacts through successive scattered and massive immigration, publication exchanges, media (Radio Marti and TV Marti), plays, and visits by Cuban artists to the U.S., mostly outside Miami. Inside Cuba, information about the U.S. and Cuban Americans arrived more frequently, through annual visits by tens of thousands of Cuban Americans and others, the internet, and radios sent or brought to the island. Cubans have also sought unofficial information on their own; garage shops in Havana for several years built and sold parabolic antennas to Cubans interested in watching TV produced outside Cuba; also, enterprising Cubans made clandestine internet connections from a server reaching multiple users through hidden cables stretching throughout some Havana neighborhoods. Both initiatives attempted to overcome Cuba's ban on universal internet use and on TV programs from abroad. They reveal Cubans' interest in the outside world and their ingenuity in circumventing government-controlled information.

Traditional Cuban culture brings Cuban Americans and Cuban residents closer to each other. The Buena Vista Social Club phenomenon impacted U.S.-born Cuban Americans as much as recent Cuban arrivals to the U.S. Celia Cruz was and will remain an icon to all Cuban Americans and Cuban islanders alike. Newcomers incorporate the music of Willy Chirino, an idol of Cuban American culture, while still cherishing the rhythms of revolutionary Cuba's artists. Recent arrivals become American baseball fans while reading, in Spanish, Cuba's baseball league scores in the sports pages of Miami-Dade's newspaper.

On this shore of the Florida straits, non-political songs composed in the Castro era now play in clubs and functions in Miami-Dade and other cities where anti-Castro political culture is evident. Likewise, Cuban CDs produced in today's Cuba appear in most Latin music shops. These songs are often associated with the feelings, life experiences, and rites of passage of young Cuban Americans who grew up in communist Cuba. So are the slang and buzzwords prevalent in today's Cuba, which are heard more and more where Cuban Americans congregate. Even the proper names of many young arrivals such as Mileysis or Dosvelys (at times the fusion of two words into one with an ever-present "y") contrast with the Marias, Robertos, and Patricias—names commonly given to the sons and daughters of early exiles.

More than half of all Cuban Americans did not live in pre-Castro Cuba. Many of those who left Cuba in their childhood years have at best indirect knowledge of the events that occurred from Castro's Moncada Garrison assault in 1953 to the flight of Fulgencio Batista on December 31, 1958. Likewise, few Cuban Americans have formally studied or read about the island's republican era, either because they were born in the U.S. or because Cuba's government has not disseminated information about pre-Castro Cuba or portrayed it impartially. Because of this knowledge gap, it is not surprising that Cuban American culture, especially in areas of high Cuban American concentration, is slowly but surely integrating the cultural experiences of new arrivals with the norms, mores, and historical perspective of the first exile waves. These three sources should remain the primary influence of Cuban American culture for another decade or two.

SOURCES AND SUGGESTED READINGS

Alex Abella, *The Killings of the Saints* (New York: Penguin, 1991).
"Affluence in Two Cultures," *Hispanic Business,* December 2004.

Alejandro Armengol, "El Nuevo Exilio," *El Nuevo Herald*, 11 de mayo del 2004.

"Chinese Pin Hopes on Leader's Visit," *Miami Herald*, 22 November 2004.

Lesley Clark, "Hialeah Entre las Ciudades Mas Conservadoras," *El Nuevo Herald*, 12 de agosto del 2005.

Efrén Córdova, ed., *40 Años de Revolución: El Legado de Castro* (Miami: Ediciones Universal, 1999).

Daniel De Vise and Elaine Del Valle, "The Balseros/10 Years Later," *Miami Herald*, 22 August 2004.

Guarioné M. Díaz, ed., *Evaluation and Identification of Policy Issues in the Cuban Community* (Miami: Cuban National Planning Council Inc., 1980).

Cristóbal Díaz Ayala, *Música Cubana Del Areyto a la Nueva Trova* (San Juan, Puerto Rico: Editorial Cubanacan, 1981).

"Elegido Galeno de Origen Cubano Como Presidente de los Psiquiatras Americanos," *Diario Las América*, 6 de abril del 2005.

Himilce Esteve, *Exilio Cubano en Puerto Rico: Su Impacto Socio-Político, 1959-1983* (San Juan, Puerto Rico: 1984).

Cristina Garcia, *Dreaming in Cuban* (New York: Ballantine, 1993).

Pando Miguel Gonzalez, ed., *Greater Miami: Spirit of Cuban Enterprise* (Fort Lauderdale, Fla.: Copperfield Publications Inc., 1996).

Susan D. Greenbaum, *Afro-Cubans in Ybor City* (Gainesville: University Press of Florida, 1986).

Susan D. Greenbaum, *More Than Black: Afro-Cubans in Tampa* (Gainesville: University Press of Florida, 2002).

Evelio Grillo, *Black Cuban, Black American* (Houston: Arte Publico Press, 2000).

Herencia, Vol. 9, No.1, Primavera 2003.

Herencia, Vol. 11, 2 November 2005.

Oscar Hijuelos, *The Mambro Kings Play Songs of Love* (New York: Harper, 1990).

Antonio Jorge, Jaime Suchlicki, and Adolfo Leyva de Varona, *Cuban Exiles in Florida: Their Presence and Contribution* (Miami: Graduate School of International Studies, University of Miami, 1991).

"Land of Opportunities," *U.S. News and World Report*, 20 June 2005.

Lisandro Perez, "Immigrant Economic Adjustment and Family Organization: The Cuban Success Story Reexamined," *International Migration Review*, Vol. XX, No. 1 (Florida International University, 1986).

A. Portes, ed., *The New Second Generation* (New York: Russell Sage Foundation, 1996).

A. Portes and R. L. Bach, *Latin Journey: Cuban and Mexican Immigrants in the United States* (Berkeley: University of California Press, 1985).

A. Portes and A. Stepick, *City on the Edge: The Transformation of Miami* (Berkeley: University of California Press, 1993).

Rafael J. Probias and Lourdes Casal, *The Cuban Minority in the U.S.: Preliminary Report on Need Identification and Program Evaluation* (Boca Raton: Florida Atlantic University, 1973).

"Revista Hispano Cubana" *Primavera,* mayo-julio 1998.

Gerardo Reyes, "La Guerra que Posada Carriles No Pudo Ganarle a Fidel Castro," *El Nuevo Herald,* 15 de mayo del 2005.

Gloria Ruiz Quitan, "Valora el Voto La Comunidad Cubana," *El Nuevo Día,* San Juan, Puerto Rico, 19 de octubre del 2004.

Narrey San Martin, "'Dollarization' Keeping Cuba Afloat," *Miami Herald,* 1 September 2003.

Mercedes C. Sandoval, *Mariel and Cuban National Identity* (Miami: Editorial SIBI, 1985).

Eladio Secades, *Las Mejores Estampas de Secades* (Medina Hermanos, S.A., México 9, D.F., 1969).

Georgia Tasher, "First the Cigars, Now the Dogs," *Chicago Tribune,* 28 September 2003.

VI

FRATERNAL AND RELIGIOUS CONTINUITY

In pre-Castro's vibrant civil society, religious and fraternal groups were part and parcel of Cuban culture and social life. A brief history of these groups and their exodus from Cuba is essential for understanding their role in the development of traditional culture and of Cuban American culture.

During the first years of the Cuban Revolution, the conquering party viewed religious and fraternal groups and associations as inherently anti-government. The revolution showed hostility toward religious groups and institutions, along with their class-related values, that influenced Cuba's educational and economic life. The government's harassment of religious and independent fraternal associations occurred frequently and varied only in tactics, intensity, and timing.

CATHOLICS

Catholicism has been the predominant organized religion in Cuba, before and after Castro's revolution. In 1959, almost three out of four Cubans were Catholic. Rooted in the early colonization and conversion of Cuba's natives by Spanish priests and friars, Catholicism survived Cuba's wars of independence, when most Catholic clergy were Spaniards and Spain had vowed to fight Cuban independence "to the last man (soldier) and the last peseta (dollar)." In Castro's Cuba, the Catholic Church continues to host the largest number of followers, serves as the pre-eminent non-governmental humanitarian institution in Cuba, and breeds lay leaders with deep-seated religious and democratic convictions. Incidentally, Fidel Castro, the son of a wealthy family in Cuba's Oriente Province, received his high school diploma at Belen, an elite Jesuit Catholic school attended mostly by upper- and middle-class students. As a group, Catholic lay leaders were among the first to oppose the revolution, and their clergy the first expelled or forced out of Cuba by Castro. Most Catholic clergy left the island by 1963. Many prominent Catholic lay leaders who opposed Castro were executed and imprisoned in Cuba while others played leadership roles in the Bay of Pigs invasion and subsequent anti-Castro activities. These Catholic leaders came from diverse social backgrounds and included students, landowners, industrialists, professionals, clergy, and the faithful at large. Most belonged to Cuba's middle and upper social strata. Before 1959, the Catholic Church served as a vital institution in the education of Cuba's upper and middle classes, and in other humanitarian endeavors. In that year, there were 200 Catholic schools with an enrollment of 62,000 students; 2 Catholic universities; 1 meteorological observatory; 1 boy's town for abandoned children; 22 asylums for elderly care; 3 hospitals for the care of females; 1 hospital for the care of lepers; and 2 clinics for the treatment of the mentally ill.

The Catholic Church played a key role in the early exodus of Cubans to the U.S. The Catholic Refugee Assistance Program assisted most Cubans arriving to the U.S. between 1959 and 1972. And the American Catholic Church, in tandem with Catholics in Cuba, planned and carried out the exodus of some 14,000 unaccompanied minors popularly known as the "Peter Pans."

Soon after their arrival in Miami, Cuban Catholics congregated in parishes located in their host neighborhoods (Little Havana, Westchester, Hialeah, and Coral Gables) and eventually throughout Miami-Dade County. In fact, about half of today's Dade Catholics (800,000) are of Cuban ancestry and have been a key factor in the growth of Catholicism in South Florida. During the 1960s, Cuban American Catholics gathered at religious services in churches in New York, New Jersey, Los Angeles, and other cities where Cubans first settled. The ranks of Cuban American Catholic clergy have included bishops in Florida, New York, and Texas. Cuban Americans have founded or helped found Catholic institutions in South Florida, among them St. Thomas University, Belen Jesuit Preparatory School, the Southeast Pastoral Institute, the San Juan Bosco Church, and the Ermita de la Caridad del Cobre (shrine to Cuba's patron saint, the Virgin of Charity). Every September 8, thousands of Cuban Americans participate in masses and processions honoring Cuba's patron saint, or "cachita," a term of endearment occasionally used by Cuban American Catholics.

By the 1980s, and especially in Miami-Dade, tens of thousands of Cuban Catholics were praying together—often in Spanish masses officiated by Cuban American priests—sending their children to Catholic schools with large numbers of Cuban American students, celebrating annual reunions of pre-Castro Catholic school alumni, founding schools and pastoral institutes, ordaining Cuban American bishops and high church officials, and later they helped arrange the Pope's visit to Cuba in 1991. In recent years, Cuban American Catholics have provided financial aid to thousands of the elderly along with the frail and needy still living in Cuba, and they have re-established personal and institutional ties with their counterparts on the island.

After decades of government hostility toward religious practices, Pope John Paul II was allowed to visit Cuba. He rekindled religious values and beliefs among many Catholics and instilled them in others. Despite government barriers, more young Cubans are becoming involved in religious activities, not only in churches and temples but also in religious processions and lay activities in Cuba's towns and cities. For several years these religious groups and institutions have received financial and in-kind assistance from Cuban Americans.

HEBREWS

As a group, Cuban Hebrews were among the first to leave Cuba. When revolutionaries seized power in 1959, approximately 12,000 Jews lived on the island—about 40 percent of them Sephardic.

Most Cuban Hebrew families settled in Cuba between the 1920s and the 1940s from countries like Germany, Russia, Poland, and other Nazi-occupied countries. They were a visible part of Havana's trade and commercial establishments and produced a growing number of second-generation teachers and other professionals. Their community included forty-seven different organizations throughout the island, for example, synagogues, an orphanage, and civic and cultural groups like Centro Israelita Guanabacoa and Union de Oriundos de Lituania. First-generation Cuban Hebrews involved their children in Jewish institutional life and transmitted their heritage and traditions to their offspring. Both first-generation European Hebrews carrying traumatic personal experiences of the Russian Revolution or the Holocaust and their Cuban-born offspring quickly fled Castro's revolution. By 1962, about 90 percent had reached the U.S. and became an integral part of the first wave of Cuban American refugees. Like other Cubans, most Cuban Hebrews (70 percent) settled in Miami, and some 15 percent went to New York's metropolitan area.

Once in Miami, first-generation Cuban Jews formed their own associations, notably the synagogue Cuban-Hebrew Congregation, the Interamerican Hadassak, and the Cuban-Hebrew Circle. Over the years, most second- and third-generation Cuban American Hebrews have integrated into American Jewish institutions, religious and others. While a numerically small proportion of the Cuban American Diaspora, Cuban American Hebrews are prominent among Miami's civic, economic, and political leaders, the media, and other fields. Since their arrival to the U.S., Cuban American Hebrews have actively supported Israeli causes and leaned toward conservative religious practices.

PROTESTANTS

In 1959, 6 percent of Cubans were Protestants, mostly Baptists who lived in the provinces. Protestants operated one hundred schools located throughout the island, most of them Methodist and Presbyterian.

Protestant churches in pre-Castro Cuba had special cultural ties to the U.S. dating back to the sixteenth century, when French and English Corsairs, filibusters, and pirates raided and seized areas of Cuba.

In the eighteenth century, the British briefly took Cuba's eastern city of Guantanamo and occupied Havana and other western areas for one year. While there, they exercised significant influence on the island's commercial and religious practices. By the nineteenth century and beyond, the influence of the U.S. and its Protestant ethic in Cuba was undeniable, especially in the aftermath of the Spanish-Cuban American War. A massive evangelization movement led by U.S. pastors and ministers sparked growth of Protestantism on the island.

Like other Cuban religious and cultural groups, historical Protestants—Methodists, Episcopalians, and Baptists—left Cuba in large numbers between 1960 and 1962. After 1980, other denominations followed in large numbers—Disciples of Christ, Pentecostals, and Seventh Day Adventists. In 1983, Miami-Dade hosted 191 organized Hispanic Protestant churches, mostly Cuban American with a combined membership of 80,000. By 1990, most of the active Protestants who had lived in Cuba in 1959 had left the island and settled in the U.S. Protestant service agencies played a major role in the resettlement of Cuban refugees, especially during the 1960s. In 1990, there were 10,000 Cuban American Baptists in South Florida and 90 Baptist churches in Miami-Dade alone. Also, the county hosted more than 55 predominantly Cuban American Congregationalists, 2,000 Methodists, a similar number of Presbyterians, about 5,000 Adventists, several thousand Jehovah's Witnesses, and a few hundred Mormons.

Today, almost one of every five Cuban Americans belongs to a Protestant denomination. By and large, Cuban American Protestants are integrated into the Cuban American community, both residentially and institutionally. They have settled mostly in Miami, New York, New Jersey, and other Cuban American enclaves, starting or joining churches and congregations with a strong Cuban American membership. Cuban American Protestants support their brethren in Cuba and share the political views of most Cuban Americans, serving as members of civic and patriotic organizations. Dozens of Cuban American pastors and ministers shepherd not only Cuban American congregations but also more diverse flocks, such as the one in Florida ministered by a Cuban American Episcopalian Bishop. A Cuban American leads the Washington, D.C., church where U.S. presidents pray and are counseled before their swearing-in ceremony.

MASONS

The Masons are one of the oldest and most important fraternal institutions in Cuba's history. The first-known Cuban Masonic loggia, Discreción, was founded on the island in 1861. One hundred years earlier, Masonic rites were held in Cuba during the one-year occupation of Havana by an English fleet.

As members of secret patriotic societies, Cuban Masons served as civilian and military leaders in Cuba's wars of independence from Spain in the nineteenth century. Masonic loggias functioned in Cuba as fraternal secret societies that believed in a supreme being called the Universe Grand Architect and espoused the principles of liberty, equality, and fraternity. By 1958, the number of Cuban loggias had grown to 342 (60 in Havana) and were present in all of Cuba's 126 municipalities, where they wielded extensive influence. These loggias, grouped under the Gran Logia de Cuba (Cuba's Grand Loggia), practiced the Scottish Rite and totaled some 40,000 Cuban Masons and paramasons, including the Hijas de Acacia (Acacia's Daughters) auxiliary organization. After 1959, Masonic leaders started leaving Cuba more gradually than Catholics, Jews, or Protestants. Since 1959, about half of Cuba's Masonic leaders have left the island. The Cuban Revolution did not conduct a major anti-Mason offensive until 1968, when loggias' documents and assets were confiscated and fines exacted on loggia members. Today, fewer than 300 loggias remain in Cuba, with an active roster of some 12,000 members. These societies have less influence on Cuba's social life than they did during the pre-Castro era, when Masons owned and managed a university, museum, and insurance companies, and claimed some of the island's top political and cultural leaders.

Following a 1960 initial gathering of 200 exiled Cuban Masons, the first Cuban loggia in exile—Libertad Igualdad y Fraternidad (Liberty, Equality and Fraternity)—was formed in Miami. Subsequently, Cuban American Masonic leaders continued founding their own loggias in the U.S., some independent from both Cuba's and other U.S. loggias. Over time, the U.S. hosted five Cuban American Grand Loggias, namely, Gran Logia de la Lengua Española (Spanish Language Grand Loggia), Gran Logia de Cuba (Cuba's Grand Loggia), Gran Logia Antillas (Antilles Grand Loggia), Federacion de Masones Exilados (Federation of Exiled Masons), and Cuba Primero (Cuba First), the latter with affiliated loggias in New Jersey, New York, Philadelphia, Chicago, Tampa, Hialeah, Miami, and Los Angeles. By the end of 2004, about fifty Cuban American loggias existed, while other Cuban American Masons functioned under U.S. Masonic jurisdictions. Some Cuban American loggias maintain informal humanitarian ties with loggias still active in Cuba.

Historically, there have been Cuban American Masons who also have identified themselves as Catholic, Santeros, Protestant, or as members of other religious groups. About half of the offspring of exiled Masons in Miami remain active in Cuban American loggias.

SOURCES AND SUGGESTED READINGS

Alvaro Alva, "Presencia Judia en Cuba," *Diario Las Americas,* 10 de diciembre del 2005.

Rene De La Vega, *Influencia de la Masonería en la Historia de Cuba* (Miami: December 2000).

Antonio Jorge, Jaime Suchlicki, and Adolfo Leyva de Varona, *Cuban Exiles in Florida: Their Presence and Contribution* (Miami: Graduate School of International Studies, University of Miami, 1991).

La Voz Católica, *Nuestro Primer Obispo: Don Luís Peñalver y Cárdenas* (Miami: 2005).

Marcos A. Ramos, *Protestantism and Revolution in Cuba* (Miami: Research Institute For Cuban Studies, Graduate School of International Studies, University of Miami, 1989).

Armando Salas-Amaro, *Ajefista y Masón* (Miami: 2003).

Armando Salas-Amaro, *El Secreto de la Logia* (Miami: 2003).

Armando Salas-Amaro, *José Marti, Maestro Masón: Antonio Maceo, Hombre o Titán* (Miami: 2004).

VII

POLITICS

POLITICAL CULTURE

Most Cuban arrivals in the 1960s settled in Miami, where an active political culture soon developed and continues evolving to this day. Early anti-communist exile culture focused almost entirely on Castro's overthrow, a prompt return of exiles to Cuba, and the preservation and/or restoration (in Cuba) of traditional pre-Castro values, institutions, and the 1940 constitution.

During the early 1960s, exiles did not prescribe establishing roots in American society. They anticipated a short stay in power for Castro and longed to return to, and restore, their way of life in pre-Castro Cuba.

But after the first ten years in exile, Cuban Americans saw little hope for a quick return to a free Cuba. Around the late 1960s and early 1970s, Cubans began to prepare psychologically, culturally, and materially for life in America. Gradually, living in the U.S., be it Miami or elsewhere, set the tone of today's Cuban American culture. Enclaves in Florida, New York, and New Jersey—and to a lesser extent in Illinois, California, and Massachusetts—saw the rise of businesses and professional practices, media outlets and publications, publishing houses, and art galleries. These institutions fostered the development of a shared Cuban American political culture based in the U.S. but carrying a strong interest in the old country.

Cuban American politics in Miami have temporary as well as long-term features. The focus includes issues like the representation of Cuban Americans in government and White House and Congressional policies that relate to Cuba, i.e., the treatment of Cuban boat rafters by the U.S. government. The Cuban American community becomes more prominent in American public opinion when occasional controversies like the Elian Gonzalez saga or massive unplanned immigration arise.

PERCEPTIONS AND REALITIES

Cuban American politics has orientations beyond the typical U.S. partisan or ideological politics. It can be a mix of American political conservatism and a twentieth-century Latin American populism lingering in the exile community's memory of pre-Castro Cuba. When one listens to Miami's Spanish talk radio, it is not uncommon to hear hosts and telephone callers espousing politically conservative views such as tax cuts, school vouchers, and reduced government while defending populist liberal social causes such as a higher minimum wage, government responsibility to help the needy, better workers' benefits, and protection of the underdog against greedy big business.

Another example of the ideological dichotomy is electoral politics in Hialeah, a municipality in northwest Miami-Dade County that counts the largest number of Cuban Americans of any U.S. city. In 2005, the City of Hialeah was ranked the fourth most conservative city in the U.S. Yet, for decades, Hialeah voters, most of them Cuban Americans, elected and re-elected an outspoken democrat as their mayor until he retired that same year.

INTERGROUP RELATIONS

The post-Castro migration of Cubans into the U.S. unfolded at different times and under different social environments and historical circumstances than those of other Hispanic American groups. For instance, Mexican Americans in Texas and other states were legally bound and socially pressured to abandon the culture and traditions of their ancestors.

In these U.S. communities, Hispanic children endured punishment for speaking Spanish in public schools. The practice caused many Hispanic parents to strongly encourage their children to speak English only and to join non-Hispanic White social groups and institutions as a means to avoid prejudice and discrimination.

Before the 1970s, U.S. Hispanics were a small minority in most urban centers and did not have enough votes to empower themselves as significant voting blocs. Also, they included large numbers of low-income individuals with limited English and education. In those days, and with notable exceptions, Hispanic professionals and entrepreneurs pursued success outside of Hispanic enclaves and institutions. This began to change with the late fifties and sixties civil rights legislation that increased the access of minorities to educational resources and federally financed anti-poverty programs. After 1980, the Hispanic middle class grew significantly in the U.S., as immigrants from Latin America included more professionals and better-educated individuals in their ranks.

The early experience of Cuban Americans differed from that of other Hispanics and led to the early creation of their own community-based social, cultural, and economic institutions.

For instance, the first wave of Cuban exiles included a large group from Cuba's former upper and middle classes; they did not consider themselves minorities, were unfamiliar with the history of U.S. minorities, and felt nothing but gratitude for the U.S. for providing temporary refuge, as they hoped for a quick return to a free Cuba.

The trauma inflicted on exiles by the Cuban Revolution, particularly in its early years, contributed to the exile community's world view and made them highly suspicious of drastic social change, abuse of government powers, class and racial strife, and criticism of the U.S., the country that offered a new life of their choice. The turmoil exiles had experienced in Cuba distanced them from the

American social movements of the 1960s, such as civil rights, women's liberation, and opposition to the war in Vietnam, causes then popular among U.S. minorities and many social groups.

Conversely, some U.S. leaders of the 1960s, fed by Cuba's revolutionary propaganda machine, labeled all Cuban Americans as followers of Cuba's former dictator Batista, racists, corrupt elites, and oligarchs who opposed Castro out of greed and self-interest. Most U.S. Hispanic leaders of the 1960s perceived—rightly so—that early Cuban exiles were detached from U.S. Hispanic concerns such as civil rights, guest-worker border issues, and poverty. The disconnect between early Cuban émigrés and other Hispanic leaders was geographic as well, because most Cuban Americans living in Florida rarely traveled out of state.

Although a handful of Cuban American groups, like the Cuban American National Council, established close working relationships with Mexicans and Puerto Ricans in the early 1970s, not until the 1980s and beyond did most Cuban American and other Hispanic leaders and groups begin exploring their common interests and interacting with each other. Factors included the fast growth of the middle and upper classes of Mexicans and Puerto Ricans, the arrival of new waves of Cubans, political changes occurring in the U.S., mutual business interests, and the mass arrival of Hispanic immigrants from several Central American, South American, and Caribbean countries.

PUBLIC PERCEPTION OF CUBAN AMERICANS

In the early 1960s, when Cuban Americans began to arrive in the U.S. in large numbers in a legal, planned, and orderly fashion, American public opinion was favorable toward Cuban immigrants. The newcomers had a reputation as successful professionals and entrepreneurs and arrived after a wave of Hungarians, who settled in the U.S. in the late 1950s with success.

By the late 1970s, America's public opinion against mass immigration, legal or illegal, was growing. Enter Mariel, when the Cuban government handpicked a relatively small number of criminals, and an even smaller number of others with serious physical illnesses or mental disorders, and shipped them to Miami among a large improvised flotilla of 125,000. The episode changed the golden image of exiles and the Cuban community as a whole; public opinion previously viewed the community as middle- and upper-class, mostly White, religious, law-abiding families who had lost their homeland fleeing communism.

Other Miami-specific factors affected the perception of Cuban Americans. In the 1980s, voters in Miami elected Cuban Americans to public office in growing numbers. Because Cuban politics and national origin have recurred as campaign issues for Cuban American candidates in Miami-Dade County, Cuban Americans were often perceived by others as single-issue politicians with only a marginal interest in domestic affairs. Florida's non-Hispanic White political establishment and non-Cuban American voters viewed them as political newcomers. Cuban Americans running as Democrats received no support from their party in primaries. For years, it was all but impossible for Cuban Americans, or Hispanics for that matter, to win the Democratic nomination in districts without a Cuban American majority of voters. A Cuban American Democrat selected as state chairman in 1975 served as a notable exception; he played a major role in attracting Cuban American voters to the presidential campaign of Jimmy Carter.

Widespread negative feelings for Cuban Americans in Dade County pervaded non-partisan events as well. In 1980, the county passed an antibilingual ordinance mostly backed by non-Hispanic Whites who felt that the growing proportion of Miami-Dade Hispanics threatened their jobs and lifestyles.

The involvement of a few criminals in well-publicized drug-smuggling cases, bombings, and other crimes in the late 1970s and 1980s also influenced public perception of Cuban Americans. These acts were attributed to or committed by a handful of Cuban Americans against federal government offices in Miami and other Cuban Americans whose political views the perpetrators opposed.

The 1980s also included non-criminal but nonetheless controversial incidents in Miami involving public protests of theater plays and pop concerts. The media and non-Cuban Americans often portrayed and perceived the views and actions expressed in the protests as attempts to stifle U.S. freedom of speech rights. Thus, what many Cuban Americans considered a good way to show their unyielding opposition to Castro's travesties had the unintended consequence of alienating important sectors of the American public.

The most recent, and perhaps most publicized example of differing perceptions between Cuban Americans and others was the Elian Gonzalez saga.

Elian Gonzalez was five years old in late 1999 when his mother drowned in the Florida Straits trying to escape Cuba in a small boat, a vessel that carried other escapees, most of whom also died. Elian miraculously survived afloat for many hours before two fishermen rescued him. Eventually brought to Miami, he received care from his uncle, cousin, and other relatives. For Cuban Americans, he was a living symbol of Castro's oppression and of the lost lives of Cuban escapees. Elian's mother was divorced when she left Cuba, and the child's father soon claimed custody. Elian became an instant political symbol for the Cuban government, who demanded his return to his father in Cuba, an action that most Americans found reasonable according to parental rights. A legal process reaching the U.S. Supreme Court resulted in Elian's return to Cuba after U.S. law enforcement agents, dressed in full combat gear and with assault weapons, tear-gassed the house of Elian's relatives, extracted the child, and initiated his return to Cuba.

Elian's custody dispute proved again the salient role that Cuban Americans often play in American life despite their numbers—they represent less than 1 percent of the U.S. population. Arguably, events related to Elian's return to Cuba influenced the Democratic Party's lukewarm political support for a Cuban American senatorial candidate in Florida who, as Dade County mayor, publicly refused to cooperate with federal authorities pursuing physical custody of the child.

The handling of Elian's case had other ramifications. It likely contributed to limiting the political future of the then U.S. attorney general; swayed enough Cuban American votes in a presidential election eventually decided within Florida by just a few hundred votes; and prompted Miami's current mayor, inspired by Elian's forceful predawn extraction, to run for office. On the verge of the 2000 presidential election, an estimated 2,000 Cuban American Democrats turned Republican; another 3,000 Cuban Americans, individuals who had registered as independents or had crossed parties to vote for Bill Clinton, did not vote for Al Gore.

The Elian Gonzalez case was a high-profile example of differing perceptions between Cuban Americans and broad sectors of Americans. While opinion polls showed that, for most Americans unfamiliar with Cuban issues, Elian's return to Cuba was a simple exercise of parental rights, for Cuban Americans, it denied a child freedom and happiness and condemned him to a deprived life in communist Cuba.

To most Cuban Americans in Miami-Dade, Elian became a symbol of patriotism, a hero representing a cause they could rally around. And rally they did. Thousands of Cuban Americans marched, held vigils, and discussed Elian with deep-seated emotion expressed on a large and unprecedented scale. Extensive support for Elian staying in the U.S. came not just from Cuban American activists. Marches and prayer meetings included grandmothers not used to long walks anywhere, and rallying family members spanned three generations of Cuban Americans. Miami's Spanish-language radio covered events and protests surrounding Elian's saga daily, and soon a visible number of non-Cuban Hispanics joined the Cuban American community in support of the cause.

In the aftermath of Elian's *cause célèbre,* differences between Cuban Americans and others popped up again in the 2000 Miami-Dade County mayoral race, when an unknown non-Hispanic White candidate rode an anti-Cuban backlash to third place with 20 percent of the vote, despite his minimal campaign spending.

BLOC VOTING AND ELECTING CANDIDATES

Cuban American political influence in the U.S. is a function of the community's concentration in South Florida, Miami-Dade in particular; the proportion of registered Cuban American voters and their high voting turnout; the exodus of non-Hispanic White voters from Miami-Dade County; voting patterns favoring Cuban American candidates; in response to candidates who seek the Cuban American vote; and early alignment with Florida's Republican Party when it had few incumbents and Florida residents began showing more moderate-to-conservative voting patterns. In the mid-1970s, Cuban Americans represented only 8 percent of Miami-Dade County registered voters. In those days, Cuban American community leaders and opinion makers still discussed whether becoming a U.S. citizen to gain political influence was unpatriotic. By the end of the decade, Cuban Americans began to run for and win local elections—mayoral and city council—in districts with large numbers of Cuban American registered voters.

In 1980, they voted in record numbers for Ronald Reagan, while also electing a Democrat as the first Cuban American occupant of a county-wide seat on the Miami-Dade School Board. Following a decision by Florida's Supreme Court on single-district representation, three Cuban American Republicans gained election to Florida's state legislature. By 1984, it was clear that Cuban Americans made up an important if not decisive voting bloc and that they had begun to change Florida's political equation.

A review of Cuban American voting preferences in 1976, 1996, and 2000 shows increases in the percentage of Cuban American votes that went Democrat. In the late seventies, when a Cuban American headed the Florida campaign of then-presidential-candidate Jimmy Carter, Democrats received about a third of the Cuban American vote, despite the fact that a majority of Cuban Americans had voted in greater numbers for President Nixon a few years earlier. A similar phenomenon occurred in 1996 when about 40 percent of Cuban Americans voted for President Clinton, who actively reached out for the Cuban American vote in the Miami area. The opposite

resulted when Vice President Gore faced Election Day in Miami in the aftermath of the Elian Gonzalez incident and received just one of every five Cuban American votes.

History shows that while Cuban American registered voters predominantly lean Republican, their vote is elastic enough to reflect variations in candidates' positions and party policies. Their tendencies are important enough to influence the outcome of close elections in Florida and nationwide, as the 2000 election results showed.

Cuban American participation in the American political system has not dwindled since the mid-1980s, when eight out of ten Cuban American registered voters actually voted. In the first half of that decade, the proportion of Cuban Americans registered to vote increased by 5 percentage points and the proportion of actual voters by 8 percent.

By the time Richard Nixon became president in 1972, Cuban Americans had clearly aligned with the Republican Party. As Florida became a more conservative, pivotal state in national elections, Cuban Americans seized the opportunity to seek political office as Republican candidates. By the mid-1970s, a sizable Cuban American population concentrated in Miami-Dade County (more than 300,000) were becoming U.S. citizens (20 percent); two thirds were registered to vote but still constituted less than 10 percent of all Miami-Dade registered voters. In 1980, three of every four Cuban Americans were registered Republicans, and almost all of them voted along party lines. They were among the first voting blocs that composed America's broad-based support for Ronald Reagan. President Reagan's political victories in Florida accompanied a 7 percent increase in the number of Cuban American registered Republicans, and an equal decrease in the number of Cuban American registered Democrats. In two consecutive national elections, 90 percent of the Cuban vote went Republican, a rate unsurpassed by any candidate of either party. Incidentally, Reagan was the first president in U.S. history to have lunch with a large group of Cuban American leaders in a family restaurant, located in the little Havana neighborhood of

Miami, and owned by a Cuban American. His outreach to the Cuban American community also included the appointment of Cuban Americans to high federal posts such as assistant to the president for Latin American affairs, ambassadors to Venezuela, Guatemala, and the United Nations. It came with open support for anti-Castro political causes dear to many Cuban Americans. Henceforth, Cuban Americans have continued to gain statewide and national representation by backing candidates perceived as anti-Castro and who take time to visit with Cuban Americans in Miami-Dade County.

By 1992, Cuban Americans made up one third of Miami-Dade County registered voters and almost half of all Dade County Republicans. In less than a decade, the proportion of all Florida Democrats and Republicans in the State House reversed. By 2002, Republicans had gained thirty seats, and Cuban Americans composed a majority of Dade County Republicans. Likewise, in the State Senate, Florida Republicans showed a majority gain of nine seats in that year.

In 2005, Cuban Americans from Florida had three members of Congress—Ileana Ros-Lehtinen and Lincoln and Mario Diaz-Balart—and a U.S. senator, Mel Martinez, a former cabinet member. Also, Cuban Americans boasted nine state representatives, one of them slated to become the first Hispanic speaker of the house; three state senators; five mayors; thirty-eight elected members of legislative bodies in Miami-Dade; four members of the Miami-Dade County Public Schools Board; and five Cuban American judges elected to the county court, the court of appeals, and the circuit court. In Broward County, Florida, a Cuban American had served as county mayor and remained a member of the county commission. Cuban Americans won elections to legislatures in the states of Kansas and Delaware, and a Cuban American became mayor of Wichita. Bob Menendez, a Cuban American congressmen from New Jersey who was named the third-highest-ranking member of the Democratic Party in Congress, became a U.S. senator in 2005. He was a former mayor, former state senator, and state assemblyman. Following in his footsteps, another rising Cuban American Democrat served both as mayor of West New

York and speaker of the New Jersey Assembly and was elected to the
U.S. congressional seat previously held by Senator Menendez.

EVOLVING CUBAN POLITICS

Most Cuban Americans oppose Castro, disagree with his policies, or
believe his time to step down is overdue. Nonetheless, anti-Castro
politics among Cuban Americans have evolved in the last four
decades. Among other things, U.S.-born Cuban Americans are not
exiles, as much as they may identify with them. Political exiles and
refugees are now fewer than they were in the 1960s, and the sporadic
violence practiced by a handful of Cuban Americans against other
Cuban Americans perceived as Castro sympathizers has virtually
disappeared since the 1980s.

Likewise, trips to Cuba by U.S. Cubans, whether for
humanitarian reasons or otherwise, were inconceivable in the early
1960s. By 2004, about 100,000 U.S. Cubans visited the island every
year, and travel agencies arranging the trips advertised on local TV,
newspapers, and Spanish-language radio stations in Miami-Dade
and elsewhere. That same year, President Bush restricted travel to
the island by Cuban Americans and the amount of money they
could remit to Cuba, limiting transfers to close relatives. By then
the Economic Commission for Latin America (ECLAC) and others
estimated at $800 million to $1 billion the amount of money
received by Cubans annually from Cuban Americans, both via
remittances to friends and relatives in Cuba and delivered personally
during trips to the island.

Reaction to the new restrictions show internal differences
among Cuban Americans based on their date of arrival to the U.S.
It underscores the complexity of Cuba-related issues after forty or
more years of Castro's regime. In general, recently arrived Cuban
Americans favor a more liberal policy on travel and remittances to
the island than Cuban Americans who have resided in the U.S. for
decades, especially those who opposed Castro actively or suffered
the regime's violence. Recent arrivals are also more likely than their

Cuban American predecessors to have close relatives in Cuba and to come to the U.S. for socio-economic reasons instead of the political ones that motivated early exiles.

It remains of interest that the new travel policy strengthened the U.S. embargo on Cuba at a point when food and medicine sales to Cuba by American businesses had reached their pinnacle since 1960.

Most Cuban American groups generally support the embargo and would like to see Castro's regime end. They differ, though, on whether the political and economic isolation of Cuba should preclude humanitarian considerations, which affect their relatives on the island.

For Cuban Americans, opposition to Castro has a different meaning than it did in the 1960s. Such feelings and ideological or patriotic views now find expression through the activities of political, cultural, professional, social, economic, patriotic, or regional organizations; in efforts seeking to involve the international community; in the promotion of human rights; in the support of dissidents in Cuba; participation in TV shows, conferences, and events that involve discussion of Cuba; book publications and articles; plays, movies, and documentaries; vigils, hunger strikes, and ecumenical events. Years ago, these activities were secondary and seen mostly as vehicles in support of military or forceful opposition to Castro. Another and more familiar example of today's Cuban American politics is the advocacy by Cuban American members of Congress of anti-Castro measures. Their efforts on the Hill exemplify the insertion of politics by Cuban Americans in today's American foreign policy vis-à-vis Cuba. Overall, Cuban Americans are shifting the focus of opposition to Castro from military actions by exiles to U.S.-led political and human rights initiatives and to the aid of internal opposition on the island. In both cases, the anti-Castro paradigm slowly makes its way from Miami to Cuba.

As in any other large community, the majority of Cuban Americans are not political activists. On the other hand, a changing but pervasive anti-Castro political culture has transcended generations and birthplace. Media sympathetic to Cuban Americans and to active community-based groups, especially in Miami and the northeast area of New Jersey, have kept it alive.

Not all Cuban Americans stay attuned to anti-Castro sentiment; the younger generation has shown little interest in trying to change circumstances in Cuba. Instead, the younger generation, whether raised in the U.S. or in Cuba, shares or ignores Cuban American political culture. Meanwhile, they wait for Castro's departure and form their own cultural nuances and adjustment mechanisms to forge a life in the U.S.

SOURCES AND SUGGESTED READINGS

Christoper P. Baker, *Cuba* (Eneryville, Calif: Moon Travel Guides, 2004).

Cuban Affairs (Princeton, N.J.: Cuban Committee for Democracy, Summer/Fall 1996).

Lesley Clark, "Hialeah Entre las Ciudades Mas Conservadoras," *El Nuevo Herald,* 12 de agosto del 2005.

Jim De Fede, "Candidate's Outsider Theme Is Losing Steam," *The Miami Herald,* 15 August 2004.

Roger Díaz De Cosió, Graciela Orozco, and Esther González, *Los Mexicanos en Estados Unidos* (Sistemas Técnicos de Edición, México, D.F., 1997).

Theodore Draper, *La Revolución de Castro, Mitos y Realidades, Segunda Edición* (México: Congreso Por la Libertad de la Cultura, agosto del 1962).

Evelio Grillo, *Black Cuban, Black American* (Houston: Arte Publico Press, 2000).

Herencia, Vol. 9, No. 1 (Coral Gables, Fla.: 2003).

Antonio Jorge, Jaime Suchlicki, and Adolfo Leyva de Varona, *Cuban Exiles in Florida: Their Presence and Contribution* (Miami: Graduate School of International Studies, University of Miami, 1991).

Naleo Educational Fund, *National Directory of Latino Elected Officials* (Los Angeles: 2002).

"New Realities May Now Count in City Politics," *New York Newsday,* 22 February 1991.

Marifeli Perez-Stable, *The Cuban Revolution, Origins, Course and Legacy* (New York: Oxford University Press, 1993).

A. Portes and R. L. Bach, *Latin Journey: Cuban and Mexican Immigrants in the United States* (Berkeley: University of California Press, 1985).

A. Portes and A. Stepick, *City on the Edge: The Transformation of Miami* (Berkeley: University of California Press, 1993).

Jorge Ramos, *The Latino Wave: How Hispanics Will Elect the New American President* (New York: Harper Collins, 2004).

Gerardo Reyes, "La Guerra que Posada Carriles No Pudo Ganarle a Fidel Castro," *El Nuevo Herald*, 15 de mayo del 2005.

Fresia Cadivid Rodriguez, "Cuban Exiles Exert Most Foreign Policy Influence," *Hispanic Link Weekly Report*, 7 October 2003.

VIII

BUSINESS AND ECONOMICS

The city of Miami is little more than a century old. Back in 1958, before Cubans began arriving in large numbers, Miami was a sleepy resort town near the better-known, glitzy Miami Beach, where *The Jackie Gleason Show* was produced and the beautiful people vacationed. For the most part, the city of Miami hosted a population of retirees and service workers. Its limited commercial and industrial operations catered mostly to tourism and local needs. At the time the local construction industry stagnated, a general recession plagued Miami, and unemployment was high, especially for minorities.

Cuban American entrepreneurs were part of the first wave of Cuban émigrés. Many of them spoke English and were familiar with American culture. One of the catalysts of Cuban American businesses sprouted in metropolitan Miami through "character" or "handshake" loans. Cuban American bank officers granted them to émigrés who had no collateral but carried reputations from pre-Castro Cuba as successful entrepreneurs or managers. Start-up loans allowed hundreds of Cuban Americans to go into business with little or no starting capital. The loans made up part of the social capital Cuban Americans brought to Miami in the early 1960s. Social capital, together with the profile of 1959 Miami, allowed penniless Cuban Americans to enhance Miami's image and role in national and international affairs.

The social capital of the first Cuban exile wave had several components that worked in tandem, sometimes deliberately and at other times serendipitously. Key among these components were trust, a sense of shared destiny, similar socio-cultural backgrounds and educational levels, shared values such as a strong belief in democracy and free enterprise, individualism, self-confidence, an affinity for the U.S. and the American way of life, and the legacy of a well-developed society that many of them had helped build.

The investment of this social capital in a young municipality with enormous potential and sufficient economic and educational infrastructure yielded—in less than a half-century—an image of Miami with a visible Cuban influence beyond U.S. borders. This settlement model had unique features worth considering.

SOCIAL CAPITAL INVESTMENT AND COMMUNITY BUILDING

The first waves of Cuban exiles and refugees concentrated in a young municipality with a progressive educational system, plenty of undeveloped land, little commercial activity or international trade, and available rental housing units. Small Cuban American families first rented and eventually bought their own homes, where they started a new life along with arriving relatives. They gravitated to neighborhoods where the signs reading "no children, no dogs, no Cubans" of the early 1960s soon disappeared, as those who had posted them soon moved out to non-Cuban areas within and outside Florida.

Probably the above environmental and demographic factors are sufficient to explain why Cuban American institutions prospered and experienced sustained growth in Miami-Dade. The decision by most Cuban American families to teach Spanish to their children—and to instill pride in their culture, native language, and community—also factored in. So did the social capital they brought, which included cultural, financial, and managerial assets invested in Cuban American neighborhoods. Barely more than a decade after their arrival, community-based professional practices and businesses provided a wide range of goods and services to thousands of Cuban Americans—and eventually to all Hispanic consumers—in a culturally familiar environment.

The investment of this social capital in turn received support from a large consumer base of tens of thousands of Cuban Americans. They purchased their goods and services, attended cultural events, and followed media with a show of solidarity that transcended class and generational lines.

And last but not least, Cuban Americans founded more than two hundred associations of various types, not to mention sports clubs and little leagues, theater companies, publications, clinics, funeral parlors, and other businesses. This community infrastructure played a significant role in attracting Latin American public officials, executives, and tourists to south Florida and promoted trade between Florida and Latin America.

Obviously, Cubans did not make Miami. The city and Dade County would have developed eventually; the real estate is valuable and the climate attractive. Regardless, the historical fact remains that Cuban Americans played a key role in the area's development. They were pivotal in Miami's role in international trade, its urban growth, its network of thousands of small businesses, and its role as a gateway to America for business, tourism, and hemispheric events. In addition, Cuban American leaders and the public at-large have played supporting and creative roles in the area's cultural events, whether in the performing, literary, or visual arts.

SUSTAINED GROWTH

Cuban American–owned businesses in the U.S. have grown exponentially since 1970, when statistics were first kept. The biggest growth in numbers took place between 1972 and 1982. The number of Cuban American–owned businesses increased sixfold, from 5,000 to more than 30,000. During the following two decades, Cuban American businesses grew by 60 percent and 66 percent respectively.

By 1997, Cuban American businesses represented 10 percent of all Hispanic-owned businesses in the U.S. Seventy-two percent of

Cuban American businesses—120,000—were located in south Florida and predominantly in the Greater Miami area. Other states with large numbers of Cuban American businesses included New York (6,000), New Jersey (5,600), California (9,000), Texas (2,600), and Illinois (1,300). The number of large and small businesses, and the revenues they generated, reflect this concentration.

Also in 1997, Cuban American businesses reached $2.7 billion in sales, or 14 percent of the total output of all Hispanic businesses in the U.S. This represented a jump from $400 million in 1972. By 1987, Cuban American businesses in the Miami area (60 percent of all Cuban American businesses) constituted the second largest Hispanic business community in the U.S. It generated more in sales than the Hispanic firms in any other metropolitan statistical area in the U.S. This achievement is notable because the Cuban American population that year represented slightly more than 5 percent of all U.S. Hispanics.

In 1997, the average revenue of all Cuban American businesses was $211,000, a figure higher than all other Hispanic firms ($155,000) but still half of the average revenue for all U.S. firms ($411,000). When compared to other large Hispanic groups, Cuban American–owned businesses had the highest receipts per person.

In 1982, Cuban American and other Hispanic businesses employed 23,000 people in Miami-Dade County; the figure increased fivefold in the next fifteen years.

Most Cuban American businesses engage in retail, construction, and service industries. Thousands of outsourced manufacturing jobs held in Miami by many Cuban exiles in the 1960s have been steadily replaced by jobs in tourism and other service industries. The service sector currently ranks third as a job source for Cuban Americans and its number of firms grows faster than those of other industries. Also, since 1980, the Greater Miami area has played host to a steady construction boom that has generated thousands of jobs.

In 1997, more than 60 percent of all Hispanic businesses in Miami-Dade (120,000) were owned by Cuban Americans, employed seven out of ten MSA Hispanic employees (26,000), and about 10 percent of all Hispanics employed in Dade County. Eighty percent of Cuban American businesses in Miami are owner operated and report no employees on their payroll.

BEYOND LOCAL ETHNIC MARKETS

The first Cuban American businesses in Miami originated in the historically Cuban neighborhoods of the 1960s—Little Havana and Hialeah. But as Cuban families who first settled in these areas became more affluent, they moved out to suburbia and to other areas that hosted middle- and upper-class neighborhoods. Many Cuban American businesses, especially those in the service sector—restaurants, small shops, clinics, insurance, etc.—followed the dispersing population and now can be found all over Miami-Dade County.

Most Cuban American businesses started out catering to Hispanic consumers and providing ethnic products. However, since the late 1980s, especially from the 1990s onward, Cuban American businesses have served a broader, more diverse clientele. as their products and services—originating in areas like South Florida and northern New Jersey—reached outside traditional neighborhoods. By the turn of the century, products like the "Cuban sandwich" or "Cuban coffee," among others, appeared on the menus of non-Cuban-owned restaurants and coffee shops throughout the U.S.

A second trend taking shape in the 1980s and 1990s was the growth and/or creation of large Cuban American-owned businesses in Florida, and in states like California, New Jersey, and Michigan. These large businesses contribute significantly to the total output of Cuban American businesses. They also demonstrate the ability of Cuban American entrepreneurs to cross over from ethnic markets, gain access to adequate financial capital, and compete with non-minority-owned businesses.

Cuban Americans are largely responsible for spearheading the sizeable growth of Miami's foreign trade with Latin America. Hispanics in Miami have served as a business link with Latin countries, such as Venezuela, Brazil, Colombia, Argentina, and others. Trade channels forged with these countries precipitated the trade boom of the 1970s and helped diminish the volatility of international trade. The Hispanic presence in Dade County also turned Miami into a popular destination, and even a second home, for Latin American travelers, who collectively represented a significant source of revenue for Cuban American businesses. Cuban American entrepreneurs, professionals, and skilled technicians have sufficient bilingual, bicultural skills to offer a variety of services and goods to visiting tourists, and businesspeople, from Spanish-speaking countries.

The Spanish media also contributes to the success of Miami's professional networks. Early Cuban American exiles brought with them the experience of owning or running 58 daily newspapers, 2 large general-circulation magazines, several literary magazines, 270 radio stations, 23 TV stations broadcasting to the largest TV audience in Latin America, and several major advertising agencies. Cuba's population in 1958 was about 6 million.

Soon after their U.S. arrival, Cuban journalists, former media owners, and administrators joined American media outlets and advertising agencies, mostly in Miami, New York, Los Angeles, Chicago, and San Juan, Puerto Rico. By the late 1970s, Cuban Americans owned several successful radio stations in Miami that were eventually sold to, or merged with, large U.S. businesses with national and international operations. By the 1980s, Cuban Americans had forged a major presence in Miami (and to a lesser extent in other markets) in the ownership, management, and operation of Spanish-language radio, TV, newspapers, and magazines. For Cuban Americans, media has served as an important rallying vehicle for political and humanitarian causes and in the preservation of Cuba's traditional culture. It has also played a major role in the growth of businesses and in the development of the overall Hispanic market.

Since the late 1970s, thousands of Florida's U.S.-licensed entrepreneurs, professionals, and skilled technicians have formed a countywide and growing network that has helped turn Miami into the third-largest Hispanic economic market in the U.S. Cuban

Americans pay millions of dollars in federal, state, and local taxes, money that directly and indirectly reaches their communities.

While most Cuban American–owned businesses report few or no employees, they have played a key role in the absorption of thousands of immigrants from Latin America. These businesses offer jobs in the service industries that do not require high skill levels or significant command of English. Without these readily available opportunities, many immigrants would be jobless and marginalized as unproductive members of society. Some Cuban Americans who arrived after 1980 have transitioned from being employees to successful entrepreneurs, large and small, in less than two decades. Such success has countered four decades of attempts by the Cuban Revolution to make the individual anti-capitalist. According to communist and Cuban Revolutionary doctrine, this ideal, referred to as the "new man," would not seek personal gain or property.

ROLE IN INTERNATIONAL TRADE

Among the early exiles of the 1960s were former Cuban business owners and managers who for years had worked with Latin America for Cuban or U.S. companies. Upon arriving in the U.S., these individuals re-established their Latin American business contacts, first on behalf of U.S. corporations and eventually as entrepreneurs.

Cuban American businesses and professional practices, particularly those in Miami-Dade County, play a pivotal role in creating opportunities between the U.S. and Latin America (and more recently between the U.S. and Europe). For decades, Cuban Americans traveled frequently to Latin America on business and joined business delegations to the region. Over the years, Cuban Americans in Miami have organized the largest hemispheric congresses of chambers of commerce. They have included Latin American business leaders and high-level government representatives from almost every country in Latin America. Cuban American business leaders played an important role in the organization of the first Free Trade Agreement of the Americas. Held in Miami, the event gathered presidents, ministers, and other senior officials from Latin America and the U.S. Cuban Americans have presided over the Greater Miami Chamber of Commerce Board of Directors, and one became its first Cuban American CEO in 2004.

Because of the ability of large Cuban American businesses to grow and to transcend boundaries, Miami has become the third-largest Hispanic market in the U.S. Although most Cuban American businesses are small and medium in size, eighteen Cuban American–owned businesses claim annual revenues of more than $100 million each; they bring in more than $6 billion annually. Some Cuban American–owned companies are publicly traded, as their products and services—including food, clothing, real estate, and telecommunications—are widely distributed and used throughout the U.S.

CHAPTER VIII SOURCES AND SUGGESTED READINGS

"Affluence in Two Cultures," *Hispanic Business,* December 2003.

Luís J. Botifoll, *Como Se Creo La Nueva Imagen de Miami* (Miami: Consejo Nacional Cubano de Planificación, 1984).

Alexander Franco, *Business Opportunities in a Free Cuba* (Miami: Hallmark Press, 1995).

Pando Miguel Gonzalez, ed., *Greater Miami: Spirit of Cuban Enterprise* (Fort Lauderdale, Fla.: Cooperfield Publications Inc., 1996).

"Hispanic Business 500 Directory," *Hispanic Business,* June 2004.

Edward Iwante, "Immigrant Businesses Can Have Wide Economic Impact," *USA Today,* 16 November 2005.

Antonio Jorge, Jaime Suchlicki, and Adolfo Leyva de Varona, *Cuban Exiles in Florida: Their Presence and Contribution* (Miami: Graduate School of International Studies, University of Miami, 1991).

"Land of Opportunities," *U.S. News and World Report,* 20 June 2005.

Waldo Lopez-Aqueres, *An Overview of Latino-Owned Business in the 1990s* (Los Angeles: The Tomas Rivera Policy Institute, 2000).

A. Portes and A. Stepick, *City on the Edge: The Transformation of Miami* (Berkeley: University of California Press, 1993).

A. Portes and Richard Schauffler, *Language and the Second Generation* (Baltimore: The John Hopkins University Press, 1993).

Narrey San Martin, "'Dollarization' Keeping Cuba Afloat," *The Miami Herald,* 1 September 2003.

U.S. Bureau of the Census, *Hispanic 1997* (Washington, D.C.: 1997 Economic Census, Survey of Minority-Owned Business Enterprises, Company Statistics Series, 2001).

U.S. Small Business Administration, *Minorities in Business, 2001* (Washington, D.C.: Office of Advocacy, U.S. Small Business Administration, 2001).

IX

POSTSCRIPT TO THE FUTURE

DO CUBAN AMERICANS AND HISPANICS BELONG IN THE U.S.?

The preceding chapters have addressed the overall adjustment of Cuban Americans to American society through a multitude of topics. Numerous examples indicate that, on balance, their adjustment has been positive, despite events like the two massive unplanned migratory episodes and occasional acts of violence committed by a relatively small number of Cuban Americans. These events, nevertheless, have raised questions in American public opinion about the success of Cuban Americans' assimilation. The answers depend on how one defines assimilation. One school of thought believes that well-assimilated immigrants must relinquish their native language and customs, marry outside their group, speak only English to their children, maintain marginal contacts with the old country, adopt prevailing U.S. national and local mainstream agendas, and become self-reliant through traditional American economic institutions. Under these terms, Cuban Americans may not fit the mold, not completely anyway, and certainly not the way Europeans assimilated to American society in the nineteenth and early twentieth centuries.

On the other hand, it would be hard to consider marginal, dependent, maladjusted, or un-American for that matter a group of immigrants who show high naturalization rates (60 percent of Cuban Americans are U.S. citizens), labor force participation, voter registration, and voter turnout; that has formed tens of thousands of successful businesses, contributed top corporate leaders and government officials, high-ranking officers and veterans to the U.S. military; and that has shown a salient presence—disproportionate to their numbers—in just about every aspect of American life. Through four decades of settlement in the U.S., recent Cuban American immigrants have become productive members in their respective communities and reached socio-economic levels close to non-Hispanic Whites, depending mostly on place of birth, level of education reached, and years spent in the U.S.

One-third of all Cuban Americans were born in the U.S. Also born in America was an even larger proportion of Puerto Ricans and Mexican Americans; these groups have made major contributions to the U.S., not only as veterans and distinguished members of the armed forces but also as governors (Bill Richardson of New Mexico), cabinet members (Henry Cisneros), U.S. surgeon generals (Antonia Novello), and star entertainers (Rita Moreno and Jennifer Lopez).

The successful adjustment of Cuban Americans to American society has possessed unique features. For instance, Cuban Americans have not severed their family, emotional, and cultural ties with Cuba, and they have retained a keen interest in the island's present and future political affairs. They have learned English while passing on their native Spanish to their U.S.-born, predominantly English-speaking children. But what of the future of these Cuban Americans once Fidel Castro is no longer Cuba's leader?

Today's Cuba Under Castro

It is almost impossible to look at Cuba's future unless one understands certain realities—the role Fidel Castro plays in the island's governance and the reasons why Cubans have lost hope in a future under Castro. From 1959 to date, Fidel Castro has ruled Cuba. The Cuban communist party is the only legal political party, and it controls the executive, legislative, and judicial branches of government, none of them independent entities. As President,

Fidel Castro is the head of state. He is also the first secretary of the governing communist party, presides over the Council of Ministers, and serves as the armed forces (FAR) Commander in Chief. Occasionally, Castro assumes direct control of other government entities and of trivial functions, like the selection of the winner of the Miss Cuba pageant (he has also been known to prescribe the way Cuban women should cook their meals). For forty-seven years Castro has forcefully eliminated or ostracized his enemies and opponents. As recently as 2005, Fidel publicly reiterated there would be no changes in the ways of the revolution or even small steps toward capitalism. Because of the government's repression, Cubans have failed to change Cuba's social system and the flawed economic policies that continue to lower the population's living standards. Consequently, many Cubans see emigration as the best coping mechanism for dealing with unmet needs and expectations.

For most Cubans, fleeing the island is no easy task. Attempts to leave Cuba, legally or not, result in hardships (loss of employment, ration cards, etc.) or life endangerment for those who sail into the Straits of Florida in makeshift rafts. But what are some of the reasons why so many Cubans take such risks?

For more than four decades, Cubans have been asked to endure food shortages, to watch foreign tourists gain access to hotels, beaches, and other public places where Cuban nationals are not allowed, to attend countless day-long rallies, to watch endless political roundtable TV shows, and in general to put aside their hopes and dreams of a better life for the sake of the revolution. Toward the end of the last century, new generations of Cubans began to complain publicly about non-political issues, such as housing conditions, food distribution, and general living standards in socialist Cuba. Also, scores of dissidents and opposition leaders organized independent groups and associations, feats that often landed them in jail. In these cases, the incarcerated had merely been exercising freedoms guaranteed in the Universal Declaration of Human Rights, adopted by the member countries of the United Nations, including Cuba, in 1948. But such acts of individual courage have not occurred on a large scale, and from Castro's assumption of power to date, Cubans have been "voting with their feet," as their fleeing Cuba is often characterized.

THE FAILED "NEW MAN"

Decades ago, the Cuban government set out to raise "a new man," a generation of young Cubans fully committed to the revolution's ideals. In recent years, those leaving the island are these young Cubans, who represent more than half of the island's population. Born after the Cuban Revolution began in 1959, they have no personal memories of the pre-Castro era. They have demonstrated a clear preference for emigrating instead of waiting to rebuild a post-Castro Cuba, which could take an undetermined number of years. The new arrivals of this generation feel they have already sacrificed enough, yearn to plan for their future, and had grown tired of waiting for better times. One question seldom asked is why those youth were unhappy in a society that provides basic food, education, and health care above the levels of many third-world countries in Africa, Asia, and Latin America. Another question worth asking: why do these youth expect and yearn for living standards similar to those of developed countries, especially after the Cuban government subjects its citizens to constant propaganda that promotes Cuban living standards and filters out information about Western standards?

I believe that at least part of the answer lies on the fact that by the 1950s, pre-Castro society, described in previous chapters, enjoyed a standard of living similar to or above most post-World War II Western societies and rivaled U.S. standards. True, not all Cubans enjoyed those living standards. But for the many who did, those standards were expected and were transmitted to new post-Revolution generations. Beyond that, traditional Cuban individualism and the innately human desire to achieve make it hard for today's youth to accept that government leaders and tourists can drive new cars, enjoy personal luxuries, and use recreational facilities that the average

Cuban cannot experience. As they see little short-term hope, today's youth and others show a willingness to face enormous obstacles to improve their lot in the U.S., where in less than ten years, most Cuban arrivals starts a new and eventually prosperous life.

Despite the difficulties involved in leaving Cuba, legally and illegally, almost 200,000 Cubans registered for the first visa lottery (bombo) at the U.S. interest section in Havana. Another 400,000 registered in 1996, and more than half a million did in 1998.

CUBA AFTER FIDEL

There is a clear tendency among Cubanologists and those opposing Fidel Castro to expect significant changes in Cuban society once Castro relinquishes leadership altogether. Based on the history of the Cuban Revolution and its present relations with the U.S. and other nations, I share this tendency when discussing scenarios for significant change. The term *significant* is key to qualifying scenarios because societies are not static. For decades, Cuba has experienced changes in international relations, standard of living, the historical memory of different generations, its immigration policies, and other areas. Notwithstanding these peripheral changes, the central issue concerning Cuban Americans is whether there will be systemic changes in today's leadership, political structures, legal framework, and the economy of the island.

Future macrosocial scenarios are always uncertain and subject to unpredictable events. I believe, though, that the three that follow constitute likely possibilities, ones that would impact Cuban Americans and their relations with the island beyond family visits and remittances.

The first—the overnight scenario—is most easily described and analyzed. It is by far what most Cuban Americans and others hope for. Here, shortly after Fidel's absence, the state would move quickly to restore all human and civil rights; allow political parties and a free press; restore the independence of the three branches of government; depoliticize public education; adopt a market economy; legalize private property; improve relations with the U.S. as a close partner and neighbor; restore civil society institutions; free political prisoners; and, generally speaking, build a democracy with a new or revised constitution and implement a system that applies laws equally and fairly by a new set of selected leaders. This model would change Cuba so comprehensively that a return to Castro's socialism would be unthinkable.

A second possibility following Fidel's absence might be called a transition scenario. Within this model, some of the above changes would take place, but more gradually and perhaps aided by some of Cuba's present leaders. Changes would occur in Cuba's socialist constitution and possibly under communist party control. Political groups nonetheless would have the right to represent opposing views to the government within a new political framework.

It is likely that in this scenario Cuba would improve relations with the U.S. and relax current travel restrictions on Cubans. Economic changes toward a more rational economy, including private property, would occur before political reforms, but in the short term the state likely would retain control of key economic sectors. American tourism would be courted and less restricted, and U.S. investments would receive welcome under attractive terms. Some segments of the civil society—especially the religious segment, state welfare, and cultural institutions—would gain some access to media broadcasts and would be allowed to hold public events.

The third scenario is usually referred to as the succession scenario. Raul Castro, Fidel's brother and heir designee, would retain a multiyear stranglehold on Cuba's power structures—the Armed Forces (FAR), the communist party (PCC), and key economic sectors—essentially keeping Fidel's model of governance. This is the least probable scenario for several reasons. Raul is just a few years younger than Fidel and seems to lack his brother's shrewdness, charisma, and survival skills. Raul has always existed under Fidel's substantial shadow. He is Cuba's number two in every post to Fidel's number one. His willful designation by Fidel as Cuba's future leader—uncontested as of now—may not be as popular once Fidel ceases rule of Cuba; young revolutionaries, dissidents, and opponents may vie to govern the island. In addition, Cuba after Fidel will receive pressure from the European Union and other countries to open up and normalize Cuba's failed economic system.

At this point, I hasten to add that regardless of who governs after Fidel, Fidel's leadership model and style will be impossible to replicate or retain. This means that even if the succession model is adopted, it would soon develop features similar to those in the transition model, especially as the Cuban political paradigm moves toward permitting a more open society. Also, any of the three models is bound to accelerate the replacement of the older, "historic" civilian and military leaders who have helped Fidel Castro shape the Cuban Revolution since 1959. The process should bring about a more collegial and institutional leadership model.

The above scenarios neglect to consider many key issues facing Cuba's future, such as the island's public health system, family-based medical care, the role of mass organizations in an open democratic society, and the handling of claims by former owners of properties confiscated by the revolution. While these and other issues lie far beyond the scope of this book, they will affect the stability and well-being of post-Castro Cuba and, thus, should stand among the primary concerns of those wielding power.

Likewise, it is difficult to anticipate which scenario will result in the U.S. lifting or modifying its embargo on Cuba. The impact on other laws and policies adopted in the U.S. during the Castro years remains unknown as well.

WILL CUBANS RETURN TO POST-CASTRO'S CUBA?

The three preceding post-Castro scenarios suggest that relations between Cuba and the U.S. and between Cuban Americans and the Cuban's new leaders will not worsen. In fact, they may improve, depending on which scenario occurs and how it unfolds.

If any of the three do come to pass, one can consider the options open to Cuban Americans in a post-Castro era with respect to the island and to their lives in the U.S.

Most Cuban Americans, particularly those living in metropolitan Miami, will be happy to see Fidel Castro depart his post. Does that mean they will return to Cuba? Or conversely, will even more Cubans try to reach the U.S.? For years, Miami-Dade's government and civic leaders have worked in tandem with state and federal agencies to plan for orderly celebrations, uncontrolled and illegal U.S.-Cuba maritime trafficking of goods and people, and other contingencies, particularly in the event of sudden, fluid regime change.

On the other hand, not much is said about what the Cuban American community will look or sound like after Fidel. Instead, most of the attention focuses on the role Cuban Americans might play in post-Castro Cuba—as investors, politicians, tourists, returnees, or the like.

To fathom the future of Cuban Americans, one should consider both their current profile and how their community has evolved over the last four decades. The demography of Cuban Americans shows that not all qualify as exiles, at least not as historical exiles (as the media often refers to them) or as the "golden" exiles of the 1960s studied by Professor Alejandro Portes. At best, the latter now account for 20 percent of Cuban Americans, are already in their senior years or close to them, and have deep roots in America through family, social, and economic ties.

For instance, it is improbable that thousands of U.S.-born and/or raised Cuban Americans—elected and appointed public officials, corporate executives, professionals, and artists—will uproot themselves from their American milieu to adopt an entirely new life in an evolving country facing enormous challenges. Moreover, tens of thousands of Cuban American families have lived in the U.S. for many years and/or have U.S.-born children and grandchildren who will remain in America, their country, no matter what happens in post-Castro Cuba. Even Cuban Americans with weaker U.S. roots will face considerable struggles should they decide to establish permanent residency in post-Castro Cuba. Even a more open, friendlier government—with the help of massive foreign aid from the U.S., the international community, and Cuban American investors and professionals—nonetheless will need time to turn Cuba's present economy, culture, society, and politics into a form acceptable to Cuban Americans. Leaving the U.S. means finding new doctors, hospitals, housing, neighbors, friends, community resources, and conveniences not likely as available in Cuba as they are in the U.S. Also, getting used to the behaviors, idiosyncrasies, and coping mechanisms developed by Cubans to survive the ancient regime would take considerable adaptation and tolerance.

These realities, together with persistent immigration trends and the uncertainties involved in transitioning to a democratic and capitalist country, suggest that the U.S. would continue to absorb thousands of Cuban arrivals. And they will far outnumber the Cuban Americans leaving the U.S. to live more or less permanently in Cuba.

Nonetheless, one can expect that, in the short term, at least several thousand Cuban Americans will return to live in post-Castro Cuba. The various reasons include a patriotic sense of duty toward the island's reconstruction, political aspirations, family reunification, and a greater sense of belonging to a now more open, tolerant society.

MIAMI AFTER CASTRO

Events in post-Castro Cuba will have a greater impact in Miami-Dade, where most new arrivals are likely to settle, than in other Cuban American communities in the U.S. For those familiar with Miami-Dade's Spanish-language media and with the idiosyncrasies of exile politics, it is hard to imagine that Cuban Americans, particularly those remaining in South Florida, will speak with a single voice or that internal political differences among Cuban Americans will disappear through democracy. Historically, Cubans and to a lesser extent Cuban Americans have shown a greater gift for individual achievement in many spheres of life than for political accommodation for the common good. A telling phrase ingrained in the Cuban ethos, and now taken in a lighter sense, is "Estas total y absolutamente equivocado" or "You are totally and absolutely wrong." This is a popular way among many Cubans to disagree with each other that contrasts with the more sober, "I see what you are saying, but we just happen to disagree on that point." Also, Miami Cubans, not unlike respective cases of Puerto Ricans, Dominicans, Venezuelans, Colombians and others, likely will take sides with the different political forces and leaders in a post-Castro Cuba. And they will continue debating island issues through Miami's airwaves with varying degrees of passion.

Any new "rapprochement" with a post-Castro Cuba likely will result in frequent visits to the U.S. by musicians, artists, intellectuals, scientists, and others who will inject new doses of Cuba's culture into U.S. cities with high concentrations of Cuban Americans and other Latinos. From a mid- to long-term perspective, it may appear that post-Castro Cuban leaders relate to Cuban Americans in the context of twenty-first century transnational migrations. In view of this point, one should remember that even a country like Mexico with a strong nationalistic political culture allows expatriates to vote and has government offices to assist its nationals abroad. The same exists in Colombia, Nicaragua, and other countries. If this becomes the case in Cuba, Cuban politics in Miami would acquire another dimension. The next generations of Cuban Americans, especially those outside Florida, will face a challenge similar to what other Hispanic groups faced, namely the preservation of their culture and ethnic identity. Also, for a Cuban American living in Miami, increased contacts with Cubans on the island will test their sense of belonging to a broader, nationwide, Hispanic community.

For both Cuban Americans and other Hispanics, the perception of an influential Hispanic community, electorally and economically, could benefit all in spite of differing political preferences. In this regard, our own sense of belonging will help us take advantage of everyone's victories. This will influence how non-Hispanics perceive us as well.

Finally, in the social, political, economic, and psychological context of the 1960s, leaving Cuba or returning to Cuba constituted momentous steps with longer intervals of time spent in each country and less frequent contacts and communications with friends and relatives in either country. Alternatively, in a twenty-first century post-Castro environment, current information and communication technologies, accessible means of transportation, and the income levels of many Cuban Americans will not make living on either shore as final, extreme, or unlikely as it would have been during the first years of exile. And this is yet another factor to consider in our vision of the future.

CHAPTER IX SOURCES AND SUGGESTED READINGS

Narrey San Martin, "'Dollarization' Keeping Cuba Afloat," *The Miami Herald*, 1 September 2003.

APPENDIX A

DEMOGRAPHIC AND GEOGRAPHIC DISTRIBUTION

The Cuban American community is a mix of Black and White, young and old, exiles and former exiles, professionals and blue collar workers; of new immigrants seeking social freedom and economic opportunity, former Castro supporters who now live in the U.S, Cubans who lived somewhere else in the world and are now U.S. residents; and of Americans of Cuban ancestry.

NUMBER AND PLACE OF RESIDENCE

The 2000 U.S. Census counted more than 1.2 million Cuban Americans. They constitute the third largest Hispanic group in America behind Mexican Americans and Puerto Ricans. Approximately 900,000 are immigrants, and one-third are more than fifty years old. Among Cuban American respondents of the last U.S. Census, most identified themselves as White (89 percent). Almost 10 percent labeled themselves Black, and the balance did not respond to the question. Cuban Americans tend to be older than other Hispanic groups and have a greater proportion of married couples.

By the end of the twentieth century, Cuban American refugees who had arrived to the U.S. in the early 1960s represented less than one-third of all Cubans in the U.S. This group's ratio to all Cuban Americans will continue decreasing as Cuban immigration to the U.S. increases by almost a quarter-million people every ten years.

The vast majority (84 percent) of Cuban Americans live in Florida, New Jersey, California, and New York and are heavily concentrated within four of these states' large metropolitan areas; Miami-Fort Lauderdale (56 percent), New York–New Jersey–Long Island (11 percent), Los Angeles–Riverside–Orange County (4 percent), and Tampa–St. Petersburg–Clearwater (3 percent).

For instance, in 1970, half of all Cuban Americans lived in Florida, 18 percent in New York, 15 percent in New Jersey, and 9 percent in California. There were also more than 28,000 Cubans living in Puerto Rico. By the year 2000, 67 percent of Cuban Americans in the U.S. lived in Greater Miami; meanwhile, New York experienced a Cuban American population loss of 13 percent (5 percent to Miami), New Jersey lost 9 percent (6 percent to Miami), and California lost 3 percent (6 percent to Miami). Notwithstanding these trends toward concentration in Florida, a minimum of several dozen Cuban Americans live in every state, including Alaska, where Cuban sandwiches have been served to tourists. The U.S.-sponsored Cuban Resettlement Program (CRP) of the 1960s and 1970s was the main facilitator of the early dispersion of Cuban Americans over two thousand U.S. communities outside Florida at a cost of about $1 billion.

During the 1960s and early 1970s, the CRP resettled about 300,000 Cubans, mainly through services provided by four voluntary resettlement agencies. The VOLAGs program originated in the Eisenhower Administration, was fully implemented by President Kennedy, and came to a halt five years after the Freedom Flights ended in 1972. While most Cuban Americans successfully resettled in the states of New York, New Jersey, California, Illinois, Massachusetts, and Louisiana, their return flow to Miami has been evident and uninterrupted for more than two decades and has contributed to the concentration of Cuban Americans in the Greater Miami area.

The population movement of Cuban Americans contrasts with those of other Hispanic groups. While Cuban Americans tend to concentrate in and return to the greater Miami area, Mexican Americans and Puerto Ricans have dispersed from their historical concentrations. Starting off in a few states and cities, they have migrated to different U.S. communities, including places where few if any Hispanics lived before.

The 650,000-plus Cubans living today in metropolitan Miami represent slightly less than half of all Hispanics living in the area and 29 percent of Miami-Dade County's total population. For Cuban Americans, the city of Miami has been a familiar destination since it was founded in 1896, when a handful of Cuban Americans called the city home. Between 1933 and 1940, a larger group of exiles and others settled in the city, and by 1958, some 20,000 Cuban Americans resided there.

From the years 1960 to 2000, the percentage of Cuban Americans compared to Miami-Dade's total Hispanic population has declined. In 1960, Cuban Americans represented 90 percent of all Dade Hispanics. Ten years later their proportion declined to 83 percent, then to 70 percent in 1980, to 60 percent in 1990, and to 50 percent in 2000. These changes occurred because of the growing number of non-Cuban Hispanics (Nicaraguans, Colombians, Argentineans, Puerto Ricans) settling in Dade. The slower growth of Cuban American immigrants, coupled with this group's low birth rate, also contributed. Nonetheless, Cuban Americans remained the largest national Hispanic group in Miami-Dade County in 2005.

THE WORKFORCE

The income level of Cuban Americans is related to the group's occupational structure. The percentage of Cuban Americans in the workforce employed in the higher paying managerial and professional occupations (23.6 percent) ranks above other Hispanics but is still below the average for the U.S. population. The Cuban American percentage is notably influenced by second-generation Cuban Americans. One third of these U.S.–born Cubans work in managerial or professional occupations, a figure that compares favorably with 29 percent of the U.S. labor force employed in managerial and professional occupations.

The income levels of Cuban Americans vary according to their place of residence. When compared to Cuban Americans living in other U.S. areas, Cuban Americans living in Miami-Dade have a lower percentage of employees in managerial or professional occupations and a higher percentage (19 percent) of their workforce employed in lower paying jobs.

By the year 2000, the average income of all Cuban American households ($36,193) showed continued improvements. It remained below the average for the U.S. population as a whole ($40,645) but surpassed the average income for other U.S. Hispanics—$30,735.

CUBAN AMERICAN WOMEN IN THE WORKFORCE

Shortly after their U.S. arrival, Cuban American women entered the workforce and made a significant contribution to the family income. Most early Cuban exiles arrived in the U.S. with little money and few belongings. In the early days of exile, it was common for all youth and adult members of Cuban American families to hold full- or part-time jobs to help make ends meet. Most of these women held low-paying jobs delivering newspapers, parking cars, waiting tables, etc. Cuban women, many for the first time, took jobs in factories, worked as maids, and filled other service- and tourist-industry occupations.

Data on second-generation Cuban Americans suggests that exile families managed to instill in their children the value of education and the drive to succeed in life. In March 1972, more than half (54 percent) of all women of Cuban origin were in the workforce, which surpassed the rate of all U.S. women there (40 percent according to 1970 data). Currently, Cuban American women continue participating in the workforce on par with the most active female groups. Many own large- and medium-sized businesses in the fields of manufacturing, publishing, advertising, and entertainment. Likewise, there is a large proportion of Cuban American women architects, attorneys and judges, physicians, economists, accountants, and educators.

During the first years following their arrival, in the 1960s Cuban American women—about half of all Cuban refugees—showed low fertility levels compared to other population groups. During the 1980s and 1990s, Cuban American women had the highest rates, among all Hispanic American women, in the categories of women who gave birth to only one child or were childless.

POPULATION GROWTH

Cuban Americans continue experiencing a net population increase in the U.S., from 125,300 in 1960 to more than 1.3 million in 2005. The growth ratio of Miami-Dade's Cuban Americans and Hispanics in relation to non-Hispanic Whites has increased significantly since the 1970s—due in part to an outflow of 410,000 non-Hispanic Whites between 1980 and 1990, which represented a 20 percent decline.

Since 1980, the number of U.S.-born Cuban Americans has grown steadily at a rate of 5 percent every ten years. On the other hand, the Cuban American population as a whole has grown by leaps and bounds since the 1960s, mostly because of the arrival of successive large waves of Cuban immigrants. In Miami-Dade County, Cuban Americans jumped from being 21 percent of the county's population in 1980 to representing almost one in every three Miami-Dade County residents. Between 1960 and 1970, two large successive waves of Cubans increased the U.S. Cuban American population fourfold, to 544,600. The number of arrivals doubled by the next decade. Growth slowed between 1980 and 1990, despite the Mariel boatlift, which brought 125,000 Cuban "entrants" (an INS definition) to Key West. After the influx of 30,000 "balseros" (or rafters, defined as migrants by INS) brought by the coast guard to our naval base in Guantanamo in 1994 and to the U.S. a year later, most Cuban immigrants have come to the U.S. through a combination of family preference visas, the visa lottery or "el bombo," and political asylums. These represent an average of slightly more than 20,000 annually who arrived to the U.S. in regular U.S.-Cuba chartered commercial flights.

THE IMPACT OF BIRTHPLACE ON INCOME AND EDUCATION

The age and gender structures of Miami-Dade Cuban Americans are not significantly different from that of other Cuban Americans living in the rest of the U.S. The same cannot be said of other demographic aspects. For instance, Cuban Americans living in the rest of the U.S. have noticeably higher educational levels, with lower high-school dropout rates and higher college-graduation rates. Also, only 5 percent of all second-generation Cuban Americans have not completed high school, and an outstanding 43 percent of their peers twenty-five years and older have completed college. This figure surpasses not only the comparable figures for Cuban immigrants (20 percent) but also for the entire U.S. population (25 percent). In fact, educational and occupational data for second-generation Cuban Americans is similar to data for the Cuban exiles who arrived in the U.S. in the early 1960s. Cuban Americans graduate from high school (70 percent) and from college (22 percent) at rates higher than other U.S. Hispanics. However, in the year 2000, they still rated below the U.S. population as a whole.

Second-generation Cuban Americans also have higher incomes and better-paying jobs. Differences between first-generation and second-generation Cuban Americans are significant because of the impact of age on education, income, and educational levels. While half of Cuban American immigrants are older than fifty-one years, half of the second generation is younger than seventeen years; and less than 5 percent of U.S.-born Cuban Americans are more than fifty years old. Due to a combination of Cuban government regulations restricting the emigration of youth, and because of the large number of middle-aged and elderly Cubans leaving the island before 1980, first-generation Cuban Americans are older when compared to other Hispanic immigrant groups.

The younger age structure of the second generation has an impact on the group's occupational structure and income when the group is compared to first-generation Cubans and to the U.S. population as a whole. Despite the fact that older workers have seen their salaries increase over time, second-generation Cubans in the workforce have personal income levels higher than their immigrant parents. The numbers are comparable with the rest of the U.S. workforce—for instance, by the year 2000, the mean income of second-generation Cuban Americans was $40,000; the mean income of all Americans was $40,645.

Most Cuban Americans Are U.S. Citizens

One of the implications of the data presented above is that Cuban Americans have adjusted well to the U.S. Indicators beyond income and education support this argument. Naturalization rates show the desire of Cubans to become full members of American society. Since the late 1960s, Cuban Americans have become U.S. residents and citizens at a steady rate. From 1970 to 1973, the level of naturalizations of Cuban Americans remained at approximately 20,000 per year. By 1980, naturalized Cuban Americans made up 46 percent of the first-generation population. That rate increased to 50 percent in 1990 and to 57 percent by the year 2000. Not surprisingly, the majority of Cuban American immigrants living today in the U.S. are U.S. citizens. Even in the greater Miami area, which hosts the largest sociocultural concentration of Cuban Americans, the rate of naturalized citizens increased from 46 percent to 51 percent in the last decade. These rates are high when compared to those of other U.S. Hispanic American groups and to the naturalization rate for all the nation's foreign born (37 percent).

In sum, the socioeconomic situation of Cuban Americans clearly improved during the 1990s. By the end of the decade, Cuban Americans on the whole were better educated and had higher incomes and better-paying jobs than they did ten years earlier. Moreover, during the last three decades, naturalization rates and other data on Cuban Americans have reflected their positive social and economic adjustment to the U.S.

SOURCES AND SUGGESTED READINGS

Thomas D. Boswell, *A Demographic Profile of Cuban Americans,* edited by Guarione M. Diaz (Miami: The Cuban American National Council, 2002).

Thomas D. Boswell, ed., *South Florida: The Winds of Change* (Miami: 1991).

Thomas D. Boswell and Manuel Rivero, *Bibliography for the Mariel Cuban Diaspora,* edited by Guarione M. Diaz (Gainesville: University of Florida, 1988).

Lesley Clark, "Hialeah Entre Las Ciudades Mas Conservadoras," *El Nuevo Herald,* 12 de agosto del 2005.

Cuban American Policy Center, *Hispanic National Groups in Metropolitan Miami* (Miami: The Cuban American National Council, Inc., 1995).

Guarione M. Diaz, ed., *Evaluation and Identification of Policy Issues in the Cuban Community* (Miami: Cuban National Planning Council Inc., 1980).

Antonio Jorge, Jaime Suchlicki, and Adolfo Leyva de Varona, *Cuban Exiles in Florida: Their Presence and Contribution* (Miami: Graduate School of International Studies, University of Miami, 1991).

The Legislative Link, Vol. III, Issue 1 (The United Way of Florida Inc., 6 November 1992).

APPENDIX B

CUBAN AMERICAN ASSOCIATIONS

There are more than one hundred Cuban American associations and organizations in the U.S. Some are large and influential, while others are small, unlisted, and meet sporadically. Cuban American associations and organizations have different purposes such as providing social services or engaging in cultural, religious, business, or political activities.

Several organizations, such as Municipios de Cuba en el Exilio (Cuba's Municipalities in Exile), the Junta Patriotica, Cuban American National Foundation, the National Association of Cuban American Women, the Cuban American Bar Association, and others have chapters in several U.S. cities with a combined membership in the thousands. Alternatively, there are small, informal groups like the ones organized by alumni of pre-Castro private schools in Cuba who meet occasionally to reminisce about their school years.

Different religious persuasions have founded dozens of temples and organizations in Miami-Dade County. Some function independently, and others within the structure of American religious institutions. In most instances, these groups are ministered by Cuban Americans. Cuban American cultural, fraternal, and professional associations organize activities, seminars, festivals, plays, and concerts; they celebrate patriotic anniversaries; and they hold annual membership meetings.

A handful of social service organizations founded by Cuban Americans and with a majority of the latter in their governing boards receive public funds from government and other philanthropic institutions. These organizations serve the general public according to legal and programmatic eligibility criteria and have a clientele reflecting the neighborhoods' ethnic mix and the nature of the services provided.

Most Cuban American political organizations oppose Fidel Castro and espouse a near-term systemic change in Cuba's governing structures and its leaders. A few advocate for Castro's succession by Cuba's current political leaders with the hope of an evolutionary transition into more democratic institutions. Increasingly anti-Castro and/or succession politics rely on events taking place inside Cuba and on Cuba's emerging leaders. Beyond a common anti-Castro stand, Cuban American political groups have diverse strategies and agendas, and they often do not share the same political ideologies or membership profiles.

Examples of the latter are different groups formed by ex-political prisoners from Castro's jails; veterans of the 2506 Brigade; conservative business leaders; human rights advocacy groups; former and new members of pre-Castro's political parties; and members and activists of U.S. political parties. Also, there are a handful of Cuban American political groups that oppose the U.S. embargo against Cuba and seek more contact between Cuba and the U.S. In addition to their political advocacy, Cuban American political associations and coalitions host cultural, patriotic, and social events, as do virtually all Cuban American organizations.

All of the above suggest that developing a comprehensive listing and taxonomy of Cuban American associations is a complex and lengthy process that extends beyond the scope of this book.

With this in mind, I have categorized more than one hundred Cuban American associations into five groups. The groupings are based on a combination of factors such as the association's primary focus, their board composition, their name, and their founding members. Admittedly, the list is incomplete, and I look forward to adding new entries in the future. Also, some of the associations listed may fall under more than one of the five categories.

The first group includes cultural, professional, and fraternal associations. The second group consists of political and advocacy associations with a focus on issues inside Cuba, on U.S. policies toward the island, or on actions toward Cuba by the international community. Third, there is a group of associations organized around business issues in the U.S. The fourth category includes associations focused on religious issues and events particularly related to Cuba and Cuban Americans. The fifth group includes a handful of nonprofit organizations that were founded by and are governed by Cuban Americans, which deliver human, social, and advocacy services to all eligible individuals regardless of race, nationality, or any other restrictive category contemplated by U.S. law.

CULTURAL/FRATERNAL/PROFESSIONAL/ ACADEMIC

CALIFORNIA
Costa Mesa
Colegio de Farmacéuticos

Downey
Patronato José Martí

Glendale
Circulo Guinero

Inglewood
Sociedad José Martí

Los Angeles
Colegio Cubano de Periodistas
Cuban American Bar Association
Grupo Teatro Cubano del Club Cultural Cubano
Junta Cívico Militar

Monterrey Park
Club Cultural Cubano

Northridge
Patronato José Martí, Inc.

Panorama City
Colegio de Abogados Cubanos

Pasadena
Pro-Arte y Cultura

Sun Valley
Cuban American Teachers

FLORIDA
Coral Gables
Cuban Children Cancer Foundation
Cuban Cultural Heritage
Cuban Women's Club
Cuban Medical Association in Exile
Cuban American Heritage
National Association of Cuban American Woman
Operation Pedro Pan Group, Inc.
Spanish American League Against Discrimination

Jacksonville
Cuban American Club
Cuban American Cultural & Humanitarian Exchange, Inc.

Key West
Cuban American Heritage Festival

Miami
Municipios de Cuba en el Exilio
Bibliotecas Independientes de Cuba
Instituto de Estudios Cubanos
Instituto Jacques Maritain

Grupo por la Responsabilidad Social Corporativa en Cuba
Confederación Campesina de Cuba
Solidaridad de Trabajadores Cubanos
Todos Unidos
Cuban Pharmaceutical Association
Federación Masones Cubanos
Guías Espirituales del Exilio
Colegio Nacional de Abogados de Cuba
Colegio Nacional de Periodistas de Cuba
The Cuban Librarians in Exile Association
Asociación de Ingenieros Cubanos
Cuban American Endowment for the Arts
Cuban American CPA Association, Inc.
Cuban American Medical Convention
Facts About Cuban Exile
Asociación de Contadores
Circulo Nacional de Periodistas de Cuba
Colegio Nacional de Pedagogos Cubanos
Miami Medical Team Foundation
Municipios de Cuba en el Exilio
R:.L:. "Perucho Figueredo"
R:.L:. "Florencio Pino #1"
R:.L:. "Libertad"
Bmta:. Logia "Fraternidad"
R:.L:. "Armonía"
R:.L:. "Alberto Chávez"
Unión de Cubanos en el Exilio (UCE)
R:.L:. "Hijos de Conciliación"
Bmta:. Logia "Antonio de la Piedra"
Bmta:. Logia "Guáimaro en el Exilio"
R:.L:. "José Manuel Avila Acosta"
Regional Norte de la Federación de Masones Cubanos Exiliados "Cuba Primero"
Gran Logia de Cuba en el Exterior
Gran Logia Unida de las Antillas
Colegio de Notarios Públicos en el Exilio

Rotarios Cubanos en el Exilio
Cuban American Bar Association
Club San Carlos
Pen Club de Cubanos en el Exilio
Club de Leones Cubanos en el Exilio
Colegio Medico Cubano Libre
Cuban American Student Association
Alianza Fraternal Jose Marti
Cuban Museum Inc.
Sociedad Cubana de Orlando Inc.

Tampa
Casa Cuba
Centro Histórico Cultural Cubano
Club Cívico Cubano
La Unión Martí-Maceo
Logia Masónica Héroes y Mártires

West Palm Beach
Cuban American Club, Inc.
National Association of Cuban American Educators

GEORGIA
Doraville
Atlanta Cuban Club

ILLINOIS
Chicago
Cuban Association of Bilingual Teachers
Cuban Bar Association of Illinois

INDIANA
Gary
Cuban Association, Inc.

NEW JERSEY
Newark
Bmta:. Logia "Miguel Teurbe Tolón"
Bmta:. Logia "Esperanza"
R:L:. "Antonio María Castillo y Sublime"
Organizaciones Cubanas Unidas

Union City
Club Hijos y Amigos de Fomento
Pro-Cuba

NEW YORK
Flushing
Cuban American Associates

New York City
Centro Cultural Cubano de New York
Cuban Cultural Center

NORTH DAKOTA
Bowie
Circulo Cubano de Maryland

OHIO
Dayton
Cuban Association of Dayton

PENNSYLVANIA
Philadelphia
R:L:. "Máximo Gómez" - Gran Logia de Pennsylvania

TEXAS
Dallas
Cuban Catholic Committee of Dallas
Cubanos del Metroplex

Houston
Casa Cuba

Katy
Cuban American Students Association

WASHINGTON, D.C.
Cuban Democracy PAC

POLITICAL/ADVOCACY

CALIFORNIA
Arcadia
Cuban American Foundation

Los Angeles
Cuba Independiente y Democrática
Junta Cívico Militar
Brigada 2506
Cuban American Voters National Unity Committee

San Gabriel
Junta Patriótica Cubana Regional de California

FLORIDA

Miami

Coordinadora Social Demócrata
Partido Demócrata Cristiano de Cuba
Unión Liberal Cubana
Brigada 2506
Acción Democrática Cubana
Agenda Cuba
Comité Cubano Pro Derechos Humanos
Cuba Study Group
Fundación Nacional Cubano Americana
Hermanos al Rescate
Movimiento Democracia
Arco Progresista
Movimiento Cristiano Liberación
Unidad Cubana
Consejo Nacional del Presidio Político
Movimiento 30 de Noviembre
Agenda Cuba
Movimiento Demócrata Cristiano
Movimiento Democracia
Vigilia Mambisa
MAR por Cuba
Comando Martiano
Presidio Político Histórico
Unidad Cubana
Junta Patriótica Cubana
Cuba Primero
Cuban Representation of Exiles
Alpha-66
Cuban American National Foundation
Cuban American Defense League
Cuban Democratic Directorate
Cuban Committee for Democracy
Plataforma Democrática
Partido Social Demócrata

Coordinadora Social Demócrata
Unión Liberal Cubana
Partido Demócrata Cristiano-Cubano
Cuban Liberty Council
Asociación de Veteranos de Bahía de Cochinos
Unidad Cubana, Inc.
Cuban American Commission for Family Rights
Puentes Cubanos
Partido Nacionalista Cubano
Ex Club de Miami
Directorio Democrático Cubano
Cuba Free Press Inc.

Tampa
Asociación de Presos Políticos y Exiliados Cubanos
Consejo Cubano del Exilio
Movimiento Insurreccional Martiano (MIM)
Cuban Military Alliance
Junta Patriótica

INDIANA
Fort Wayne
National Federation of Cuban American Republican Women

Gary
Cuban Association, Inc.

LOUISIANA
New Orleans
Asociación de Ex-Presos Políticos Cubanos

BUSINESS

FLORIDA
Miami
Cámara de Comercio Latina-Miami
Latin Builders Association
Asociación Interamericana de Hombres de Empresa

ILLINOIS
Chicago
Cuban American Chamber of Commerce of Illinois

SOCIAL SERVICES

FLORIDA
Miami
Cuban American National Council, Inc. (CNC)
Little Havana Activities & Nutrition Center
Miami Medical Team Foundation
Liga Contra El Cancer
SALAD / Spanish American League Against Discrimination

RELIGIOUS

CALIFORNIA
South Gate
Cofradía de la Caridad del Cobre

FLORIDA
Miami
Christian Commitment Foundation
Cuban Hebrew Congregation
Caballeros de la Orden de Malta
Archicofradía de la Caridad del Cobre
Orden de los Caballeros Católicos de Colon
Amor en el Principio
Archicofradia Nuestra Señora de la Caridad del Cobre
Caballeros Católicos
Caballeros de Colón
Camino del Matrimonio
Comunidad de Vida Cristiana-Regina Mundi
Cristiandad
Encuentros Juveniles
Impactos

NEW JERSEY
Union City
Casa de la Caridad

TEXAS
Dallas
Cuban Catholics of Dallas

Appendix C

Chronology of Selected Events Affecting Cuban Emigration to the United States (1959–2004)

1959   Cuban Revolution begins. President Eisenhower establishes the Cuban Refugee Center. Fleeing Cubans are allowed to stay in the U.S.

1960   U.S. imposes a trade embargo against Cuba. Castro nationalizes assets of foreigners and Cuban nationals, and the number of émigrés increases by tens of thousands.

1961   President Eisenhower breaks diplomatic relations with Cuba. President Kennedy establishes the Cuban Refugee Program as the Immigration Act is enacted. U.S.-organized Bay of Pigs invasion fails. U.S. breaks diplomatic relations with Cuba (January 1). Large number of Cubans are allowed into the U.S. via commercial flights and from third countries. Visas are waived. Castro declares he will always be a Marxist-Leninist.

1962   U.S., Cuba, and U.S.S.R. missile crisis is resolved avoiding a super-power nuclear conflict. U.S.-Cuba commercial flights are suspended. U.S. Migration and Refugee Act provides permanent funding authorization for the Cuban Refugee Program. By year-end, 200,000 plus Cubans live in the U.S. Cuba imposes food ration card and conducts second agrarian reform land expropriations.

1963–1964 President Kennedy bans travel to Cuba and makes financial and commercial transactions with Cuba illegal for U.S. citizens. Fewer Cubans are able to leave the island through sporadic international flights to Jamaica, Mexico, and Spain. Castro faces internal opposition from anti-communists and from Soviet-backed historical Cuban communist party. Food shortages and government control of the economy, education, labor, and other institutions increase.

1965   Fidel Castro invites Cubans who wish to leave to be picked up by U.S. relatives in Cuba's Port of Camarioca: 3,000 come to the U.S. in less than two months. U.S. and Cuba sign a Memorandum of Understanding (MOU) allowing Cubans to come to the U.S. and an airlift, or freedom flights, begin.

1966   President Lyndon B. Johnson signs Public Law 89-732, the Cuban Adjustment Act, allowing over 250,000 Cubans residing in the U.S. to become permanent legal residents after one year of residing in the U.S., and without having to leave the country as part of the immigration process. Massive resettlement of Cuban Americans outside Florida begins with assistance by private voluntary agencies. Also, potential dependents on government assistance (elderly, disabled) are allowed to become residents without a financial affidavit. One hundred twenty-three thousand Cubans apply for permanent residence in the U.S.

1966–1970 Freedom flights trickle down after bringing just over 250,000 Cubans into the U.S. as the Cuban Adjustment Act becomes effective.

1968   Remaining private sector in Cuba is nationalized, and mobilization of urban residents to work on agricultural production increases.

1969   Castro announces the rationing of sugar.

1972   Freedom Flights end.

1973   Phase out of the Cuban Refugee Program begins.

1974–1977 Naturalization rates of Cuban Americans steadily increase.

1977   U.S. government lifts prohibition on travel to Cuba. U.S. and Cuba open Interest Sections in each capital.

1978   Fidel Castro invites and hosts a group of about one hundred Cuban Americans to visit Cuba who engage in a dialogue with government officials.

1979   Following the 1978 dialogue in Havana, about 7,000 political prisoners and their families are allowed by Cuban government to leave for the U.S. Also between 1979 and 1980, about 100,000 Cuban Americans are allowed by the Cuban government to visit their relatives on the island.

1980   Ten thousand Cubans storm the Peruvian Embassy in Havana and seek political asylum. Fidel Castro invites all Cubans who want to leave the country to be picked up by Cuban American relatives in the Port of Mariel. One hundred twenty-five thousand Cubans come to the U.S. in an informal flotilla of vessels, large and small. Cuba's Vice President Carlos R. Rodriguez meets secretly in Mexico with U.S. Secretary of State Alexander M. Haig. Fascell-Stone Amendment makes

Mariel refugees eligible for U.S. federal aid. President Jimmie Carter orders a blockade to stop U.S. boats from traveling to Mariel. Mariel harbor exodus is stopped in September.

1982   Charter air links between Miami and Havana are halted by the U.S. government. U.S. bans travel to Cuba by prohibiting monetary expenditures by U.S. citizens.

1984   U.S. Department of Justice decides Mariel-Cuban and Haitian refugees are eligible to legalize status and obtain eventual citizenship as previous Cuban immigrants have had since 1966. U.S.–Cuba reach agreement for the return of 2,746 undesirable Mariel refugees and the normalization of immigration processes between the two countries. U.S. agrees to grant 20,000 visas yearly to Cubans wishing to leave the island.

1985   U.S. Information Agency, news service Radio Marti begins broadcasts to Cuba. Cuba suspends immigration talks with the U.S. and abrogates 1984 agreements.

1987   Cuba restores 1984 agreement with the U.S., allowing the return of undesirable "Marielitos" to the island.

1988–1989 Soviet-block countries become independent. U.S. limits travel-related expenses for U.S. citizens to Cuba at $100 per day.

1990   Soviet Union implodes and aid to Cuba ceases. Fidel Castro declares a "special period" of shortages and sacrifices for Cubans.

1991   Soviet economic subsidies to Cuba worth over $6 billion annually end.

1992   Torricelli Act toughens Embargo against Cuba.

1994   In July, Cuban vessel "13 de marzo" carrying dozens
of unarmed Cubans seeking to flee the island is sunk
by a Cuban military patrol boat. Thirty-nine men,
women, and children drown or otherwise disappear
in the Gulf of Mexico. A month later, in a separate
incident, thousands of Cubans watch Cuban police
detain a small ferry boat manned by Cuban escapees
trying to sail from Havana Harbor into the Straits
of Florida. Witnesses become enraged and throw
stones and objects against the police and stores in the
"Malecon" (seaside wall) area of Havana. Following
the riot, Fidel Castro announces he is withdrawing
border guards and will allow those who want to leave
to do so unharmed. In just one week, thousands of
Cubans take to sea on rafts, boats, and practically
anything that floats. By August 19, President Bill
Clinton orders the Coast Guard to intercept rafters
at sea and bring them to Guantanamo to be interned
there indefinitely. Thirty thousand escapees are
brought to the U.S. Naval base in Cuba. U.S. sets a
new dryfoot/wetfoot policy allowing Cubans who
set foot on U.S. soil to stay, while returning to Cuba
those intercepted at sea. This immigration accord
with Cuba permits for the first time repatriation of
Cubans interdicted in the high seas and does not
define Cubans attempting to reach the U.S. illegally
as refugees. U.S. and Cuba reach agreement for the
admission of 20,000-plus immigrants into the U.S.
with visas. A lottery system (bombo) is established
in Havana to guarantee the availability of 20,000
émigrés. Subsequently, Fidel Castro restores the
enforcement of punishment for those attempting to
leave Cuba through unofficial means. U.S. and Cuban
officials open talks in New York City. U.S. agrees that

total legal migration to the U.S. will be a minimum of 20,000 yearly.

1996   President Clinton signs Helms-Burton legislation into law (Cuban Liberty and Democratic Solidarity Act). The Immigration Reform Act (IRA) abrogates the Cuban Adjustment Act. The act is then amended to terminate when Castro is out of power or when the president no longer deems it necessary. The president now has the power to terminate the act without Congress intervention.

1997   In September 1997, the U.S. Immigration and Nationalization Services permit Cubans who entered the U.S. through any border (sea or land) to qualify for the Cuban Adjustment Act. This eliminates the need for inspection and parole. All Cubans who had previously entered the U.S. illegally through borders with Mexico/Canada or by boat could not adjust. Previously, those who had arrived before December 1995 obtained residence through NACARA and through a 1983 amnesty. The memo from the commissioner permits thousands of Cubans in limbo to obtain L.P.S. status.

2001   Matter of Artigas, 23 I&N Dec. 99 (BIA 2001) permitted Cubans who entered the U.S. through an airport from July 1997 to present without visas (fraudulent papers, no papers, etc.) and who had been placed in court proceedings to obtain their residence through the Cuban Adjustment Act.

2004   President George W. Bush restricts visits to and remittances sent by Cuban Americans to the island. Only limited visits and amounts sent to close relatives are allowed.

APPENDIX D

CUBAN AMERICANS IN GOVERNMENT

LOCAL GOVERNMENT, 2005

MAYORS: 6

Hialeah
Raúl Martínez

Hialeah Gardens
Yioset De La Cruz

Miami
Manny Díaz

Sweetwater
Manuel Marono

West Miami
Velia Yedra Chruszcz

Wichita, Kan.
Carlos Mayans

COMMISSIONERS: 25
COUNCIL MEMBERS: 14

Bay Harbor Islands
Alberto Ruder

Coral Gables
María Anderson
Rafael "Ralph" Cabrera

Golden Beach
José M. Iglesias

Hialeah
Esteban Bovo
Vanessa Bravo
Roberto Casas
Eduardo González
Cindy Miel
Julio Robaina
José "Pepe" Yedra
   Hialeah Gardens
Luciano García, Jr.
Jorge Gutierrez
Jorge A. Merida
Rolando "Roly" Piña
Manuel Zardon
   Medley
Carlos A. Benedetto
Margarita H. De Jesús
   Miami
Angel González
Tomás Regalado
Joe Sánchez
   Miami Beach
Mattie Bower
Simón Cruz
Luis García
   Miami Springs
Peter Pacheco
   North M. Beach
Raymond F. Marin
   Sunny Isles Beach
Daniel Iglesias
   Surfside
Ruben Coto
Oreste J. Jimenez
   Sweetwater
Ariel J. Abelairas

Prisca Barreto
José Bergouignan, Jr.
José M. Díaz
Manuel Duasso
José M. Guerra
Orlando López
  West Miami
Juan Blanes
Cesar Carasa
Eduardo Muhina
Luciano Suarez

ELECTED STATE LEGISLATORS, 2005

STATE HOUSE OF REPRESENTATIVES

Delaware: 1
Rep. Joseph E. Miró (R)
Florida: 9
Rep. Rafael Arza (R)
Rep. Gustavo A. Barreiro (R)
Rep. Anitere Flores (R)
Rep. René García (R)
Rep. Marcelo Llorente (R)
Rep. Carlos López-Cantera (R)
Rep. Juan Carlos "JC" Planas (R)
Rep. Julio Robaina (R)
Rep. Marco Rubio (R)
  Georgia: 1
Ass. Sam Zamarripa (D)
  Kansas: 1
Rep. Mario Goico (R)
  New Jersey: 1
Ass. Albio Sires (D), Speaker of the Assembly

STATE SENATE
Florida: 3
Sen. Rudy García (R)
Sen. Alex Díaz de la Portilla (R)
Sen. Alex J. Villalobos (R)

ELECTED FEDERAL LEGISLATORS, 2005

U.S. HOUSE OF REPRESENTATIVES
Florida: 3
Rep. Lincoln Diaz-Balart
Rep. Mario Diaz-Balart
Rep. Ileana Ros-Lehtinen
New Jersey: 1
Rep. Robert Menendez

U.S. SENATE
Florida: 1
Sen. Mel Martinez
New Jersey: 1 (During 2004–2005 Robert Menendez served first as U.S. Member of the House of Representatives and later as U.S. Senator.)

U.S. AMBASSADORS (1980–2004)

Belgium	Paul Cejas
Guatemala	Alberto Martínez Piedra
Nicaragua–Argentina	Lino Gutierrez
Organization of American States	Luis Lauredo
Panama	Simon Ferro
United Nations	José Sorzano
United Nations	Armando Valladares
Venezuela	Otto Reich

INDEX